G000099171

DEDICATION

To our parents.

CONTENTS

ACKNOWLEDGMENTS

It's when the chips are down that you find out who your friends are and I certainly have some great friends.

CHAPTER 1:

A NEW BEGINNING.

Everything changed in an instant. One moment we were sitting around getting depressed and worrying about our future but as soon as the offer of some work came through, it suddenly felt like 'party time'.

It was as if someone had pressed a magic switch and our world had gone from winter to summer.

Driving to work the following day the whole world seemed a much better place to live in. My spirits had been lifted and I felt like a new person. I now had a six-month work contract ahead of me which would keep the money coming in. I now wouldn't need to live off my pending redundancy cheque.

I was a little disappointed that my Scottish sojourn was coming to an end. My wife Jayne and I both loved living here but without any work there was no reason to stay. It would also be nice to move back to England to be near our family and friends.

I parked my car in my usual space and walked into the factory. Everything was exactly the same as the previous day but now I had something nice to look forward to and that made all the difference. I greeted the security guard and made my way to my desk grinning from 'ear to ear'.

***

To mark the closure of the factory the company had

decided to organise a party for everyone. Interestingly they decided to hold it in a hall where they were going to supply all the drinks which they were going to buy from a supermarket.

I thought that this was a good idea and wondered why more companies didn't do this. The party was going to be on a Friday night but this created a little dilemma for me because it clashed with a Territorial Army weekend which was due to be held in Tilshead Camp on Salisbury Plain.

The TA weekend was an important one and I knew that I need to attend to ensure that I still qualified for my tax-free TA bounty payment of £900. I would have loved to go to the party but decided that I had to go on the TA weekend. This was a hard decision but I knew that it was the right one.

*

I sat in my seat on the plane to Heathrow and accepted the air hostess's kind offer of a drink from the bar. I opted for my usual Scotch and American. I kept thinking about the party that was currently 'kicking-off' in Dunblane.

I wished I could be in two places at once but knew that I had made the correct decision for all the right sensible reasons. It would have been good to have had a bit of a 'blow-out' with some of the best people I had ever worked with especially as today was my 34th birthday.

***

It had been a very long and slow five months since they had announced the closure of the factory. I still had a few weeks to go to fulfil my commitment which meant that I would qualify for a generous redundancy payment.

One good thing about not going to Munich straightaway was that it gave me some time to 'tie up a few loose ends' and say goodbye to some great people that I'd met whilst working and living in Scotland.

***

The head of the IT team in Munich contacted me to go over a few details. I got the impression that if he was aware of the sensitivity of me starting work in Munich as a contractor immediately after being made redundant from the same company in Scotland then he didn't seem bothered by it.

He confirmed that my contract would be based in Munich and would be for six months with the potential of an extension, depending on how the project went.

The project was to develop a new 'Spare Part Distribution Computer System' to replace the current 'ARE' system (Automatic Repair/Exchange) that I'd been working on in Scotland.

The project had a codename which was 'SPEED' (Spare Part Efficient European Distribution) which I thought was rather cool. I asked about my rate of pay but he didn't state an exact figure, he just said,

"Don't worry Harry, we'll cut you a good deal."

He was a little disappointed that I wasn't able to start work immediately but understood my reasons, the biggest one being that I wanted my redundancy payment.

I didn't tell him that my redundancy was worth eight months' salary which in reality was equal to a year's take-home pay as it was going be tax free. This was because it was below the tax threshold of £30,000 that the government set for such things.

Due to the fact that I wasn't going to be starting for a few weeks he said that I would need to liaise with another member of his team as he would be on holiday. I was happy with this as I could get any help that I needed from the few people I knew who already worked there.

I felt elated when I put the phone down. It was now official; I had a start date and someone to report to. All I had to do now was to figure out a way of getting to Munich and find somewhere to stay once I got there.

**

I thought about things as I drove home, six months would be great as it would give us a bit longer to sell our house and it would keep the money coming in. I didn't know how much I would be earning which was a bit strange but I wasn't that bothered as I knew it would more that I was currently earning.

Once I started in Munich, I knew that it would be two months before I would get paid as I would invoice them at the end of my first month and then they had 30 days to pay me.

I couldn't get the phrase "We'll, cut you a good deal" out of my head. What on earth did that mean? It didn't seem right to me, especially coming from an American who in my experience were tough negotiators.

***

On Saturday morning Jayne and I drove to Dunfermline with our ten-month-old son George in the back of the car. We went into a travel agent to book my flights. It was a little disappointing that there was no direct flight from Edinburgh to Munich. The girl said that I would have to change at either Manchester or Birmingham.

It turned out that Birmingham was the better option so I told her the dates I wanted and she keyed in all the details into her computer. She then turned the computer screen to show me the price.

"How much?" I exclaimed,

"That can't be right, surely. You can fly to Australia for that sort of money!"

The price she quoted me was extortionate. Jayne and I looked at each other not knowing what to say.

I realised very quickly that it just wasn't feasible for me to fly out on a Monday and return on the following Friday. I knew that I was going to be earning good money but there wouldn't be much left if I had to pay the price that they were offering.

My mouth went dry and I sat there thinking that it just wasn't going to work. The airlines had priced their tickets as if I was a rich businessman which wasn't the case. The girl returned the computer screen to its original position and keyed in some additional options. A few moments later she

4

said,

"The issue here is that you aren't staying over the weekend."

"Excuse me."

"Look, if you stayed over the weekend and flew back the following Friday then the price drops dramatically."

She turned the computer screen back to face us. The price being displayed was around £150 which was affordable. I looked at Jayne and we both knew that we had no choice. If we were going to make this work then I would have to stay in Munich every other weekend.

I turned to Jayne and said,

"The trouble is that I currently don't have any accommodation at the moment, staying in Munich at the weekend will also cost us a lot of money, especially if I have to stay in a hotel."

"But it looks like you don't have any choice," Jayne replied.

"I can see that but we won't have any money left for us at this rate."

"Look, you may as well book the ticket now and then contact your colleagues in Munich and see what they do. Someone may be able to help."

"Okay, as long as you are sure about this?"

"Yes, don't worry about us, we'll be fine. Just book the flights and we will figure a way around this somehow."

"Okay."

I turned to the girl and gave her my blue British Airways Executive Card and told her to book the flights.

"I'm afraid you don't get any discount with this card."

"I know, but if I'm flying with them, I may as well accrue some of their points."

"If you get a gold card then I know that you are entitled to enter the executive lounge."

"I think that's a long way off at the moment. I don't even have a silver card, just a blue one."

We left the shop relieved that I now had my flight tickets

sorted. However, we both realised that things weren't going to be as straightforward as we originally thought they were going to be.

***

I was feeding baby George one evening when the phone went. The caller introduced himself as the head of an IT recruitment agency. He informed me that most of the 'contractors' at the Munich site worked via his company. He then went on to tell me what the 'going rate was' and what percentage they took which was a very pleasant surprise to me after my recent experiences of 'agencies'.

He implied that his company was the 'preferred supplier' and that they did a lot of work for both for the individual contractor and the company. It all sounded very reasonable and I liked the fact that he was 'upfront' about their fees. However, I'd done all the negotiation and felt that this was 'my deal' so I didn't see why he should be involved. I thanked him for his call but politely declined his offer.

I'd learnt one very important piece of information from that phone conversation. I now knew that the hourly rate was DM120 an hour. I couldn't believe this rate, it was four times what I was currently earning, doing the same job for the same company.

Germany was obviously a more expensive place to live than Scotland and this was also a 'contractor rate'. My regular salary came with some perks such as holidays and sick pay etc. but this salary was tremendous, I just couldn't believe it.

***

In order for me to work in Munich I needed to setup a UK Limited Company. It would take too long to register a new one with Companies House as I needed to be able to trade straightaway. I found the phone number of an accountancy firm who would sell me one that they had pre-registered.

When they registered a new company, they needed to choose a name in advance. There is a risk that the names could conflict with an existing company with a similar name so they tended to make-up meaningless names. I was a little disappointed that I only had two to choose from. In the end I chose "Clayjoy Ltd".

I needed an accountant to help me with my new company's administration. The last time I used one I felt that I hadn't got a very good deal so I really wanted a recommendation from 'someone in the know'. I figured that the best people to ask were accountants so I contacted our own finance team and asked if anyone knew of one that they could recommend.

One of the accountants had a brother who was a self-employed photographer and used a 'one-man band' who was based just outside Glasgow. He said that his brother had used him for years and that he was the sort who of accountant that would fight for you. It sounded good to me so when I got his number, I gave him a call.

One evening I drove to the accountants' house and he gave me some really good advice. He made it very clear what he wanted from me. He said that I could supply the information on paper or on a spreadsheet which I could send him on a floppy disk if I wanted. This was a 'seminal moment' for me as I knew that this was the way to do it. It looked like my 'teach yourself' software training books were going to be a good investment.

It was a very good meeting and we got on very well. It was really good to get the 'ground rules' sorted out at the beginning of this business venture. It would be over a year before we needed to talk again as obviously, he was only interested in a complete year's figures. He said that due to my predicted turnover I would need to register for VAT even if I was going to be trading outside of the UK.

He also informed me that I needed to register my company with HMRC so that I would be able to pay myself. They would then send me a unique employer PAYE reference number along with a 'paying in book' which I would use to pay my tax and National Insurance. He recommended some payroll software that would do all the calculations for me.

I drove off with my head spinning. I'd been there about an hour and had taken in a lot of useful information. I knew that this was the right way to do it. However, one thing I didn't know at the time was what a fantastic asset and good friend he was going to be to us over the following decades.

***

I still felt some loyalty to the company, so after a little thought I decided that I would not charge the agency rate but would reduce so that it was the same as what I would receive after the agency 'had taken their cut'. That meant that I was now going to be earning DM105 an hour. I thought that this bit of 'good will' on my part would set the scene nicely and would contribute to the establishment of a good working relationship.

My intention was to continue to look for work in the Milton Keynes area which was where Jayne and I were from. If I was successful, we could look for a house to buy and settle down into some sort of normal family life which seemed to be so elusive for us.

***

The village where we lived was called Dollar and it had its own bank on Bridge Street, so I made an appointment to visit the manager with the aim of opening a business bank account. We chatted about things and he was a bit disappointed that I hadn't prepared a business plan but I didn't see the need to as it was just a case of going over there, doing some work and getting paid for it.

He seemed a little nervous but when he realised that I didn't' want to borrow any money he lightened up a bit. I didn't know why he'd been so worried but I could actually see the relief on his face. I didn't know what his lending criteria was, but something had been bothering him. In the end I got a good deal which included no bank charges for a year and interest on my account balance.

***

I received a phone call from a friend in Munich who said that one of their contractors had a spare room in a flat he was renting. His wife and child had been living with him but were returning to England. This was perfect for me as I would just become a lodger which would save all the hassle and expense of renting a place for myself or staying in a hotel, after all the objective was to make some money and not spend it.

Unfortunately, my new 'landlord' was not due into the office until Monday morning so I had no way of getting access to his apartment. This meant that I needed somewhere to stay on the Sunday night. I mentioned this to my 'contact' to see if he could suggest anything.

He phoned me back and said that another colleague was working in the office on the Sunday and would be able to put me up for the night. This was really good news as it would save me a lot of hassle. I knew this guy really well as he had also worked for the same American Consultancy that I had worked for in Milton Keynes, so everything was settled.

**

I still had one day left to complete the business course that I was doing in Alloa. This was a five-day course which was run by the local council with government backing. Its intention was to give some guidance to people who were thinking of starting their own business.

When I arrived at the training centre for the last day of the course, I was a bit disappointed, many of the participants hadn't turned up which made the atmosphere a little flat. However, it was an opportunity to ask lots of questions and we also had a bit of fun.

At lunch time I looked out of the window over at the same Ochil hills that I could see from the factory and sighed; I knew that 'all good things come to an end', but 'why oh why' so soon?

I took a lot away from that course. It had been a welcome change from the depressing redundancy situation

I was in. It also made me appreciate that there are people dealing with far worse conditions than I was, I wish them all well.

***

It was the last day at the factory and everyone did more socialising than working. I had lunch sitting around a table with a small group and we chatted away making small talk.

The HR manager who had helped me with the 'Munich move' joined us and promptly produced a couple of bottles of white wine and some plastic cups from a bag she was carrying. This was a very nice touch and a really good way to 'mark the occasion'.

It was all very pleasant and cordial and I felt very relaxed but we all knew that this would probably be the last time that some of us would ever see each other.

***

Walking around Stirling the following day, I realised I'd left something at the office that I wanted to keep. Each desk had its own little area which we called 'cubes', these gave a little extra privacy when you were working. There was an overhead cupboard and next to that everyone had a metal nameplate. I loved getting my nameplate as to me it was a symbol that I was officially a 'team member'.

Driving back home we decided to stop-off and see if I could get it. I chatted with the security guard and they let me in but rather unexpectedly I bumped in to my now 'ex-boss'. He asked what I was doing there and when I told him he just said that everything had been cleared away.

I looked at him disbelievingly as I thought that it was a bit quick to have done that considering that we only left yesterday. However, I decided not to 'make a scene' and just said,

"Oh, that's a shame. Never mind, it was just a thought."

I felt deep down that what he said wasn't right but I'll never know for sure. In the end we said our goodbyes and left. I was disappointed that I'd forgotten to take it with me when I had the chance as I thought that it would make a great souvenir of my time working there.

***

A TA event came up that caught my eye. There was a cross-country race to be held at a place called Penicuik. I'd heard of it before because it was where a manufacturing company was based that often advertised on the TV but I had no idea exactly where it was. It turned out to be on the outskirts of Edinburgh.

Early one Saturday morning a group of us left the TA Centre and headed towards Penicuik in the squadron mini-bus. I felt knackered and really wasn't in the mood for a race. This was 'self-inflicted' because the previous night I'd stayed at the TA centre and spent a bit too long drinking in the TA bar.

There was one soldier in the mini-bus who I didn't know. He was a young recruit, still in his teenage years. In the regular Army he would have been called a 'Sprog' due to his age. He was really keen to do well and talked tactics and techniques.

I wasn't that bothered about how we were going to perform in the race, in my view this was a good TA 'day out'; a chance to see a bit more of the beautiful Scottish countryside and claim a day's pay. However, there was also a part of me that was envious of his young enthusiasm. When I was his age, I'd have behaved in exactly the same way.

There weren't many of us but there was just enough to make up a small team. The young lad was trying to 'suss us all out' to see how good we were and I think that he thought that I was the weakest team member and I could see why. There I was, tired, hung-over and old (well, I guess at 34 I was old in his eyes).

He looked over at me and said,

"The thing is Sarge, it's important that you finish."

I looked at him for a second and thought,

"Important that I finish!'

The cocky little shit! I knew I wasn't going to have one

of my best days but I knew I was going to finish. I thought about it for a moment in my fuzzy state of mind and realised that I didn't have the energy or resources to hit back at him so I just said,

"I'll see what I can do."

I caught the mini-bus driver's eye in the rear-view mirror. He was a Staff-Sergeant and knew that I'd completed the London marathon ten months earlier. I think he expected me to hit back a bit more aggressively than that but I let it go and turned my head to continue looking out of the window.

I instantly regretted not being in better condition for this race. His comments had angered me a little but I knew I'd get around the course, I also knew that there would be some serious runners there who would have been training for months. This wasn't just a Royal Signals event but an Army event and the level of fitness in our 'front line' forces tended to be a lot better than ours.

I remembered someone saying to me once,

"If you look at a cross-country race, you'll see that most competitors run at the same pace. Therefore, you need to get to the front at the start. So many people 'hold back', thinking that they'll save themselves for later in the race but find it impossible to catch up with the leaders."

This made a lot of sense to me but to do that you needed to have a good level of fitness and a lot of confidence in your ability. I was always wary of tiring myself out too much at the beginning as I didn't want to flag at the end. On another day I might have 'gone for it' but I didn't have that competitive spirit in me today.

We all huddled in a group trying to keep as warm as we could. There was a lot of 'Squaddie banter' amongst the other runners who obviously knew each other. I decided to jog up and down in a feeble attempt at a warm-up. My head was pounding but I persevered hoping that I would feel better but I didn't, so I stopped and drank some water and re-joined my group.

The starting gun went off and there was a rush of runners all around me. My team mates also set off at a faster pace than I was prepared to do, so I let them go.

I settled into a slow jog and soon found myself running at the back of the field. I plodded on and after a while the pounding in my head subsided and feeling a bit better, I thought I would 'up my pace' a little.

My confidence grew so I focused on the runner in front of me and when I caught that person up, I would focus on the next one and so on. I was slowly making my way up the field and was beginning to enjoy myself.

I passed a runner and then looked up for the next one that I was going to 'attack'. I couldn't believe it but there in front of me was the young lad who had encouraged me to finish when we were sitting in the mini-bus. He was clearly struggling and I assume that he had gone too fast too soon.

This put a spring in my step and I really went for it. I glided up behind him and as I ran beside him, I said,

"Just remember, it's important that you finish."

I then put a spurt on that any sprinter would be proud of and I was gone.

It was not normally in my character to behave like this but I just couldn't help myself. If he hadn't said what he did in the mini-bus then I would not have been so patronising.

*

Sitting in the mini-bus, the young recruit was quiet for the whole journey back to the TA centre. I think he realised that he wasn't as good as he thought he was and was also probably a bit disappointed that an 'old git' like me had beaten him.

I didn't say anything else to him and just looked out of the window. We crossed the forth road bridge and I looked across at the famous red rail bridge. I knew that things were changing for me but one thing was for sure the beauty of this place would never change.

We arrived back at the TA Centre and I put my kit in the back of my car and drove home. I never saw that young lad again because unfortunately, that turned out to be the last day that I served in British Army.

***

CHAPTER 2:

LEAVING

It was a chilly Sunday morning when I loaded my bags into the back of the car. Jayne and I didn't speak as we drove down 'hungry hill' and out of Dollar towards Edinburgh airport. George was safely strapped into his car seat with his blanket and a toy to play with. Once on the motorway, Jayne and I started to talk about all the practicalities of my journey but not much else.

We both knew that this wasn't what we wanted but accepted that it was necessary in the short term to achieve long term stability (where had I heard that before?).

I unloaded my bags and placed them on the pavement. I kissed George and Jayne goodbye and waved vigorously as Jayne pulled away. It was a tough moment as I watched the car go out of sight. I suddenly felt very alone with an empty feeling in my stomach.

The cold winter air soon snapped me out of my malaise so I picked up my bags and hurried into the airport terminal building as quickly as I could.

I checked in at the desk and they gave me two boarding passes, one was for the flight from Edinburgh to Birmingham and the other one was for the flight from Birmingham to Munich. My bags were tagged with a Munich label so that they would automatically be placed on to the Munich flight at Birmingham.

Edinburgh airport had so many memories for me; all my hopes and dreams of starting a new life in Scotland were here and yet for the first time, I found myself flying out of the airport to go to work instead of the other way around.

I felt as if I'd gone back in time as I boarded the turboprop aircraft. It was very atmospheric with an old-fashioned romantic feel about it but on that day, for me, it was just a mode of transport.

*

I sat around the departure lounge at Birmingham Airport and looked at the front page of a large Sunday newspaper that I'd just bought. I then strolled over to the duty-free shop as I knew I was going to treat myself to a bottle of single malt but the question was which one? I spent a while browsing the good selection before making my mind up. I wanted a whisky that I hadn't had before and after a good look, I chose one which is now one of my favourites.

There was a small queue at the checkout so I waited patiently to be served. When my turn came the lady asked to see my boarding pass. She looked a little surprised when I handed it over as it was slightly different from the ones that she was used to seeing.

She looked up at me and said,

"Oh, you've got a long one there,"

Quick as a flash I retorted,

"I haven't had any complaints so far!"

It took a second before she realised what I was implying and then she lost it. The laughter gushed like a giant erupting volcano. She became hysterical and just couldn't 'keep it together'.

I was a little embarrassed as I didn't think it was that funny but eventually, she managed to control herself and continued to process my purchase. I paid by credit card and could see she had tears in her eyes when I handed back the signed chit.

She placed a plastic sleeve over the bottle and put it in a carrier bag for me.

"Thanks," I said but she just nodded at me and didn't look me in the eye.

She started to serve her next customer and I walked away. I wasn't quite sure what to make of what had just happened. One thing was for certain though; she had a really good sense of humour which was a relief.

***

They served a reasonable meal on the plane and afterwards, I asked for a 'Scotch and American dry ginger' to 'wash it down'. Looking out of the window I now realised that 'this was actually happening'. Here I was flying to Germany to go to work.

It wasn't the first time that I'd worked in Germany. When I finished my Army training, I was posted to RAF Wildenrath which was located at the western part of the country near the Dutch border. The nearest Dutch town was Roermond.

I was seventeen years old and my pay at the time, after deductions which included food and accommodation was DM 676 month. This wasn't very much but I didn't have any rank and was only a class 3 telegraphist.

This time I was now going to be earning DM 105 an hour, which meant that now I would be earning more in a day than I had been earning in a month. However, that was 17 years earlier and I obviously had to pay tax and cover my living costs.

I knew that I had a lot of expenses such as accommodation and flights but earning this amount of money would be an opportunity to 'set us up for life'. It was going to be interesting how long it was going to last, all I knew was that I would be there for six months and after that anything could happen.

The air hostess cleared my dinner items away and I ordered another Scotch and American. I poured half the scotch and half the mixer into the plastic glass and stirred it. I then sat back and I raised my plastic glass and toasted my own good fortune.

***

It wasn't long before I was collecting my bags at the carousel in Munich. It took me a little time to get my bearings as this was a brand-new airport. The last time I was there I flew into the old airport which was not too far from the office but they obviously needed to increase capacity so they built a new airport which was further out of the city. I looked around and it was immaculate.

I boarded the 'S8' S-Bahn train to Munich and as the train pulled out of the station it started to snow. I quickly realised that I hadn't bought the correct footwear as my trainers were not going to be up to the job of walking in the snow. I got off the train at Daglfing station and made my way towards the office. My route took me through a pretty little park that was next to the train track. I watched as the blue 'S8' trains went by, no amount of snow was going to delay them.

My feet were soaked by the time I got to the office. I had a coffee whilst my friend continued to work. To kill time, I went over to a pub which was just across the road. It was empty and I just sat down with a beer and watched an old Frank Sinatra movie which was in German without subtitles. It bought back fond memories of Glasgow where I saw him perform only three years earlier.

Eventually, my friend finished what he was doing and we got into his car but it turned out that he was staying at someone else's apartment who I think was his girlfriend's sister. She cooked a delicious spaghetti bolognaise and as we sat round the table enjoying it, I couldn't help thinking how surreal my situation was. Here I was, in Munich about to start work as a self-employed computer consultant. If someone had told me that a few years earlier, I wouldn't have believed them.

***

The next morning, he drove me to work. The company

was located in an anonymous office block squashed between a residential area and a main road. I was impressed that he had an electronic key to the underground carpark as I thought that parking spaces would be scarce and reserved for permanent employees.

We took the lift and I then followed his lead as we walked into a small office that contained about twelve people. The first person he introduced me to was Edward who was going to be my line manager.

"It's good to meet you in person at last Harry," he said.

"Yes indeed, it's good to be here," I replied shaking his hand.

I immediately warmed to him; he had a big smile and warm persona. We had spoken many times on the phone and had several mutual friends which helped break the ice.

He introduced me to each team member one by one. There was a sprinkling of different nationalities. They were mostly Brits with the odd American and European, I was a little surprised that not one person was German.

There was one empty desk and he said that's where I would be working. It already had a Personal Computer setup and he gave me a piece of paper which contained my logon details.

The atmosphere was very relaxed and cordial. It was interesting to meet people who I'd spoken to many times before but was now meeting for the first time. I logged on to the network with my new P.C. and promptly emailed some of my Scottish colleagues saying that I had arrived.

In the afternoon Edward introduced me to Ron who worked in a different office just down the corridor. It was Ron's apartment that I was going to be living in for the duration of my contract.

Ron had been contracting for years but I felt that the lifestyle was taking its toll on him. He was married and had a young son. His family had just returned to the UK and I felt he was a little homesick.

Once I loaded my bags into his car, he drove me back

to his apartment and as I sat in the front of his car he asked,

"One thing I forgot to ask you was do you smoke?"

"No."

"That's great; I didn't want to share with a smoker."

I was relieved that I had passed my first 'tenancy test'.

The apartment was on the fifth floor of a 1960's style block of flats in the 'Denning' area of Munich. It was basically furnished and had a well-worn feel about it. There were large south facing windows that commanded a view of some more flats.

Mine was the smallest of the two bedrooms, the contents consisted of a small bed, a chair and a wardrobe. I unpacked and went into the kitchen where Ron was preparing a pizza which he kindly offered to share.

*

We both sat at the table eating our pizza. It felt a bit strange; we were both married and both had young sons but here we were, separated from our families. It wasn't natural and not the way things were meant to be but that was the how it was for us. It is often referred to as 'the contractor's lifestyle'.

He had his own TV and decided to turn it on and we watched an American news channel which was available via cable. He turned to me and said,

"I have a video cassette player but unfortunately, I don't have any videos at the moment."

"Do UK video tapes work over here?"

"Yes, it's the same format. I think it's the American ones that don't."

"So, you can tape your own TV programs in the UK and they will work over here?"

"Yes, although it may be a bit heavy carrying a load of tapes in hand luggage."

"That's very interesting, I hadn't thought about bringing over any video tapes."

"There is an unofficial 'rental market' at work where

people swap videos amongst themselves."

"That sounds like a good idea."

***

The next day Ron drove me to the office and I studied the route carefully. I soon realised that it would be possible to walk there in a round twenty minutes which meant that I wouldn't need to rely on Ron for a lift each day.

When no one was in the office I made quick phone call to Jayne. It was good to find out that she was doing okay living alone with baby George. I decided to ask her for a favour and said,

"Can you buy me some video tapes when you are out shopping next?"

"Yes, what type?"

"VHS – E180."

"I know the 180 is the number of minutes so these are 3-hour tapes but what does the 'E' mean again?"

"I think it means extended play."

"Does that mean you can record Long Play?"

"I believe so, but don't worry about that now. Ron has a video player so I thought that you could tape some TV shows for me during the week and I could bring the tapes back out with me."

"Okay, I can do that but thinking about it, won't you need two packs of video tapes?"

"Why?"

"Because I'll need some more here when you take the first lot back with you won't I?"

"You're right, good thinking."

"Is it not worth getting the E240 as they will hold more?"

"I was told once that you get more problems with them as there is obviously more tape which makes them heavier so I'll stick with E180 if that's okay?"

"That's fine, I'll get two 5-packs of VHS video tapes for you."

"Thanks very much. That will make life more

bearable."

"Is there anything else you want?"

"Could you get me some instant noodles?"

"Instant noodles!"

"Yes please, I just want something that that I can easily make to eat."

"I see you are being as lazy in the kitchen as usual."

"It would be good to have something in, just in case I have to work late."

"So, you're eating healthily then?"

"Well, as you know I'm not into cooking and it would be good to have some English food that I like."

"You know this isn't very good for you."

"I know that but as I said it would be good to have a few things in the flat, especially if I work late and want something to eat."

"Okay, I'll see what I can do."

"Thanks, I'd better go now. I'll phone you tomorrow."

"Okay darling, love you."

It was a strange conversation but with a bit of thought and preparation I could have a bit of a better quality of life. I remembered an old Army saying,

"Any fool can be uncomfortable."

***

It was Friday morning and I watched people arriving for work carrying their bags. These were the lucky ones who were going to be flying home later in the day. There was a pleasant atmosphere and everyone seemed to be in a good mood.

It was very interesting watching people leave the office at different times to fly home. I wondered if most of them were hourly paid like me and if so, I knew that they would lose pay by leaving early. No one seem bothered, it just seemed to be accepted that this was the usual work routine.

I was feeling subdued, I really wanted to be flying home with the others. I knew that Ron was going home which meant that I would be spending my weekend alone in the apartment. There was nothing I could do about it, I just had to accept that this was my new lifestyle.

I was half expecting someone to invite me for a beer after work but it seemed that everyone who was staying had other plans.

***

I saw Ron carrying his bag so I knew he was about to leave to get his flight. He came over and said,

"Harry, as you are staying here the weekend, could you do me a favour?"

"Sure."

"Would you mind getting me some beer?"

"Sure, what sort do you want?"

"The beer I like here in Bavaria is called Helles."

"Helles?"

"It's a type of lager and is really good value if you buy it by the crate."

"Crate!"

"Yes, you'll see that they have them stacked up in the supermarket."

"Okay, I'll get some at the weekend."

"Thanks a lot, but remember that supermarkets close at lunchtime on Saturdays in Munich."

"Really."

"Yes, and they aren't open on Sundays either."

"That's interesting, so what you are saying is that I need to get up early on Saturday?"

"Well, they can be rather busy."

"Okay, thanks for letting me know."

I thought that Ron was going to ask me for a six-pack of beer, not a crate! This was going to take some carrying as the supermarket was over half a mile away. I also thought that it would have been a lot easier for him to get the beer as he had a car but I decided not to mention that.

I was planning to get some beer in for me anyway but the thought of carrying two crates back without a car would be difficult, I resigned myself to the fact that I would have to make a couple of trips.

**

I was really pleased on how my first week had gone. It felt a little strange working as a contractor when only a week earlier I was a permanent employee with the same company.

My knowledge of the local area had improved and feeling confident, I decided to take a footpath through a residential area which I thought would be a good 'short-cut'. I always preferred walking away from the road and it turned out to be a nice route that passed a pretty lake.

I began to feel a little damp sensation in my right foot. I came across a park bench and leaning against it I lifted my shoe up to take a look.

I could see that a small hole had appeared in the leather sole and I realised that it's all very well wearing nice shoes in a posh office but unfortunately, they were being destroyed by the grit that was spread on just about every footpath.

When I arrived back, I took my shoes off and I could see that both shoes now had holes in them. They were also extremely wet so I stuffed them with newspaper and left them to dry out.

**

It felt strange waking up in the apartment on Saturday morning. Normally I would be extremely busy at weekends either at home with Jayne and baby George or away with the Territory Army on exercise or training but I now had nothing to do except look after myself.

I had some cereal for breakfast and then read a bit of my book whilst drinking a hot mug of tea. Looking out of the window I could see that the weather was extremely wintery. I didn't want to go out but I also didn't want to let Ron down and as he had told me that the supermarkets close at lunchtime so I had no choice.

It was snowing slightly as I made my way along the

gritted footpath. The roads were clear and as I looked about, I could see that the Germans weren't bothered by a little 'bit of snow'.

When I arrived at the supermarket, I noticed that a mobile food stall had been setup in the carpark. It consisted of a large beige trailer and had a big serving hatch; there was a cover to give the customers some protection from the gently falling snow. I could see that it was doing a good trade as there was a small queue. I decided that I would buy my lunch there after I had got my shopping.

Walking around the supermarket I was pleased that my schoolboy German was just about good enough to allow me find what I wanted without too much difficulty. The snowy conditions created a sense of being cut-off and I felt I should stock up with every necessity. Looking around, the other shoppers were just taking the wintery conditions in their stride, this was normal to them and they were geared up to deal with it.

Some people say that Munich is the beer capital of the world and I was amazed to see such a selection. There was a small area allocated for plastic beer crates of various sizes. There were lots of them all neatly stacked together in a nice orderly fashion.

There were also a few crates that contained empty bottles that customers had returned. These were obviously going to be transported back to the beer bottling plant where they would be cleaned and reused.

I thought that it was a really good that they reused the bottles. It was far better than throwing used bottles into a 'bottle bank' where they would get smashed up. The emphasis seemed to be on reusing rather than remanufacturing which I thought was more environmentally friendly.

Looking around I spotted that there was a different design of crate. What made this crate different was that it could be split in two with each half having its own folding carrying handle. I thought that this was a brilliant idea as it meant that I would be able to carry half a crate in each hand and be perfectly balanced for the walk back.

At the checkout I put my shopping into my small rucksack and picked up my two 'half-crates' and headed towards the door. Once outside I put the beer down and pulled my coat hood over my head as it was still snowing.

I glanced over to the food trailer but rather than buy my lunch now I decided that I would take Ron's beer back to the apartment and then make a return trip. This was so that I could purchase another two 'half-crates' for me to enjoy over the weekend.

I plodded up the street carrying my heavy load. I squinted due to the bright sunlight reflecting off the white snow. I stopped a couple of times to give my arms a bit of a rest but it didn't take me long to get back where I emptied my rucksack and put my milk, cheese and ham in the fridge.

Walking back down the street I started to think about my lunch. I was delighted that I would be able to purchase something hot and cheap. One of my favourite German 'fast foods' was Currywurst which is a fried German sausage (bratwurst) and is flavoured with a mild curry ketchup. I knew that the trailers that sold these sausages were called a 'Schnellimbiss' or 'Schnelle' for short (I later found out that this term wasn't used in Bavaria).

I bought two more 'half-crates' for myself and then I made my way over to the trailer trying not to slip on the snow and ice. As I approached, I could see several rows of chickens being cooked on a huge rotisserie. There must have been about seven or so chickens squashed together on each metal skewer that was slowly going round and round.

Initially I was disappointed that they weren't selling sausages but freshly cooked chicken and chips would make a really good alternative. When my turn came, I ordered "Hanchen mit pommes" in my not very good German. I had to use my hands to indicate that I wanted a whole one rather than a half and was relieved when the lady understood me.

She removed one of the long heavy skewers, slid a chicken off the end and put the skewer back on the rack so that the remaining chickens could continue cooking. She then put the chicken in a grease proof bag and added a portion of chips.

I gave her a ten Deutschmark note, pocketed the change and put the chicken into a plastic carrier bag for extra safety. I then put this into my small rucksack trying to ensure that I kept it upright so that none of the greasy juices spilt out.

It was still snowing as I made my way back up the street. I was feeling pleased with myself having successfully completed all of my tasks. I now realised that due to the supermarkets opening times I would need to plan my weekends to ensure that I didn't run out of essential items.

***

CHAPTER 3:

SUNDAY MORNING BLUES.

Waking up on Sunday morning was a little depressing. I just didn't know what to do with myself. I made myself a mug of tea and laid in bed reading my book. Eventually I got up and had some cereal for breakfast whilst I watched some American TV.

Looking out of the window I realised that I didn't fancy going out in the snowy conditions. I was sure that the S-Bahn would be running but even if I did venture out, I didn't know where to go.

My lunch was a very simple meal. I have no interest at all in cooking and I also didn't want to make a mess in someone else's kitchen so I made up a ham salad.

Looking in the fridge I decided that I would have a beer so I picked up a bottle and poured myself a glass. I am a traditional 'real ale' drinker but I do like a cold lager either on a hot day or with a good curry. The beer was really good and I sat down on the couch switching between TV channels trying to find anything that was watchable even if I didn't understand what they were saying on the German channels.

My second beer was a real disappointment. The first one had been crystal clear but this was extremely cloudy and I really didn't like the look of it at all. I lifted it up to the light and studied it closely but I couldn't see through it.

It didn't smell like it had gone off but I couldn't make my mind up about it. I hate wasting anything, especially beer but there was no way I could risk drinking it so I decided that I had no choice and promptly poured it down the sink.

Unbelievably my next beer was also cloudy so without hesitation, I tipped that down the sink too. I was getting angry now; it had taken a lot of effort to carry the beer back from the supermarket through the snow only to find that I'd bought a bad batch.

In desperation I opened another bottle but fortunately this one was okay so I sat back down in front of the TV again and continued my search for anything watchable.

I wanted to go back to the supermarket and complain but it was Sunday and they were shut. I felt angry that I'd been ripped off but there was nothing I could do about it and even if the supermarket was open, I wouldn't know how to complain in German.

*

On Monday morning I put my trainers on to walk to work. I put my black leather shoes in my 'day-sack' as I was going to change into them once I was in the office. I also carried a spare pair of socks just in case I had to venture out into the snow at lunch time.

I was disappointed with myself that I hadn't thought about the snow when I packed my bags in Scotland. I had a really good pair of walking boots which would be perfect for walking in the snow but at least I would be able to bring them back at the weekend.

Once I was in the office, I discretely put on my leather shoes. I felt a little self-conscious walking around in them but there was nothing else I could do. It was a little bizarre that here I was, a highly paid computer consultant who was walking around the office with holes in the bottom of my shoes.

*

Sitting in the apartment later in the evening Ron produced a couple of videos that he had bought back from the UK. I chose one and put it into the video machine whilst Ron went to the kitchen area and poured himself a beer. He didn't react at all as the cloudy amber liquid filled his glass. I was just about to say something but he beat me to it,

"Good, I see you bought some Weissbier Harry," he said.

"Weissbier?" I replied, trying to sound knowledgeable.

"It's actually wheat beer, it has some sediment in it which makes it cloudy so it takes a little getting used to. Have you had it before?"

"No."

"It's very popular over here."

"Is it?"

He offered me one but I declined and made myself a mug of tea instead. Whilst my tea was brewing, I looked at the bottles of beer in the fridge. I could now see that there were two different types. I realised that I had obviously picked up half a crate of Weissbier by mistake and mixed the bottles up with the Helles lager.

Sitting down we started to watch the movie but I was more interested in watching him drink his beer. I couldn't work it out, why would anyone would want to drink cloudy beer?

***

The office block where we worked was very modern and was semi open-plan with little alcoves where small groups of employees were clustered together. This made for a pleasant working environment as it was open enough to be social but secluded to allow you to concentrate on your work.

I was walking down the main corridor and passed one of the small alcoves on my right where I overheard a conversation. I knew that this was where Ron worked,

"How's your new flat mate settling in?"

"Fine, I'm really pleased that he doesn't smoke. I didn't want to share with a smoker."

"I bet he drinks though."

"You're not wrong. He must really like Weissbier, judging by the number of empty bottles I found in the crate this morning..."

**

The time came for me to return home for the weekend which lifted my spirits enormously. Unfortunately, as I was flying back to Edinburgh, I had to leave early to ensure that I could make the connecting flight at Birmingham. This meant that I was going to earn less money but there was nothing I could do about it.

When the time came, I walked to Daglfing S-Bahn station via 'Zamilapark' which was a nice piece of 'greenbelt' land that had been preserved and made into a nice nature reserve and parkland. There was still a lot of snow around but again the footpaths had been well gritted so I didn't have any problem walking along.

The journey back home to Scotland was long and tiring but I felt a great sense of satisfaction that I'd survived my first 'stint' as a computer contractor. I was pleased that everything had gone really well and I felt that I would enjoy my new life.

*

Jayne and baby George met me at Edinburgh airport and drove me home straightaway. It felt a little strange being in a family again. Once we had dinner, we sat down to watch some TV. I was really comfortable when the doorbell rang.

When I opened the door, I could see a young girl from the village standing there. I didn't realise that Jayne had booked a babysitter. I wasn't bothered about going out but I realised that Jayne had been looking after George on her own for the two weeks I'd been away and she wanted a night out.

In the Strathallan pub we went to the bar where I ordered a pint of the local ale for myself and a lager and lime for Jayne. We then sat down and chatted with a few of the locals.

Everything seemed exactly the same as when I was last

there. The same people were drinking in the pub, the same staff were serving behind the bar and yet for me everything had changed.

"Come on then; tell me how it went?"

"Well, did you know that they drink cloudy beer in Munich now?"

"No."

"I thought it had gone off and tipped it down the sink."

"You're joking."

"Well, I didn't know it was supposed to be like that."

*

"By the way, your redundancy cheque came in the post."

"Okay, can I take a look?"

"No because I've already 'banked' it."

"Oh! I wanted to see it. It took me five long soul-destroying long months to earn that."

"I know but I didn't want to lose it so I put it in the bank straightaway."

"I suppose that was the best thing to do. I guess our friendly bank manager will be pleased."

"It's not earning much interest as it's in our current account."

"Well, we do have a lot of expenses at the moment as we are both living in two different places and these flights aren't cheap."

"So, should I leave it where it is then?"

"Yes, for the time being. I think we should let things settle down. Remember that I won't be getting paid for another six weeks or so."

"I know that but don't worry I won't spend it!"

I really wanted to see the physical cheque as I had to endure a five-month notice period to qualify for it which was part of the redundancy agreement. It had been a very long drawn out process and I was proud that I'd managed to complete it and then get some work at the end of it.

*

On Sunday morning we went to church in Tillicoultry.

We then drove back home and parked the car on the driveway before walking down the hill towards the centre of the village. Our time together was precious so rather than let Jayne cook we walked down the hill and into the 'King's Seat' pub for a nice Sunday roast for lunch.

The 'King's Seat' was on the main road and served really good food. It had been refurbished some time before and the restaurant in particular looked really smart. We placed George in a high-chair and ordered two roast lamb meals along with a couple of pints of the local ale.

We slowly sipped our beers whilst we waited for the food to arrive. I liked this pub but it wasn't one I would regularly drink in so I hadn't got to know the locals who were in the other bar.

The food was excellent and we enjoyed the pleasant atmosphere that came with busy Sunday lunchtime trade. We would both have liked to stay a bit longer but George was getting restless so we put him in his 'buggy' and made our way back up 'hungry hill' to our house.

George was asleep when we got home so we placed him in his cot. Jayne and I then made a cup of tea and watched a bit of TV before falling asleep. However, it wasn't long before George let us know that he'd had enough sleep and wanted feeding.

*

Monday came around too soon and Jayne drove me to Edinburgh airport. It was a shame that the journey took so long, having made an early start I didn't get into the office until 2:30 in the afternoon (German time). I decided to work late to make my hours up which was the last thing I wanted to do but I was here to earn money and just had to get on with it.

***

It was the end of March 1993 so I had to get my first timesheet signed. I'd taken a look at one that was supplied by one of the contracting agencies and made my own version on my P.C. I was on an hourly rate but had kept the number of hours I worked each day to 7.5 which was the normal office hours.

I hadn't completed a full month because I had agreed to work an additional week in Scotland which was the decent thing to do but now, I could see that this had affected me financially.

The next challenge was to 'raise an invoice'. Once again, I used someone else's example but as I was 'direct', this meant that I had to invoice the company and not an agency so I had to do it slightly differently. One thing that I had to do was to include my bank account details so they knew where to send the money.

Another issue for me was VAT. I'd already started the registration process but I hadn't been given a VAT number. I was worried that if I didn't charge VAT then the 'Contributions Agency' may not believe me and would make a demand for the missing VAT. I was really uncomfortable charging Vat without a VAT number as I thought that this would technically be fraud. I wrestled with this for some time.

In the end I didn't charge VAT as I was told that once I received my VAT number, I could raise a 'VAT Only Invoice' which would be for all the invoices I'd raised prior to receiving my VAT number. I really didn't like this and thought that it was very risky but this appeared to be the correct process.

I was really nervous when I asked my manager to sign my timesheet but after a quick look, he signed it without any fuss. On the way back to my desk I photocopied it and then stapled the original to my first invoice and gave it to the administrator who looked after such things.

It was as simple as that. There were a lot of 'contractors' working in the office so it was a normal procedure.

***

The next day the administrator lady came to see me with a stern look on her face.

"This timesheet is incorrect and I cannot accept it."

I was mortified and took it from her and studied it.

"Your calendar is out of sync with the days that you have worked."

I was relieved that I hadn't made a mistake with the total number of days I'd worked so it wasn't as serious as it could have been.

I apologised to the lady and said I would make another one.

"Just be a bit more careful next time and remember that we get audited so everything has to be in order."

"Okay, thanks for letting me know."

I turned and left her office. I was really annoyed with myself. This was extremely important and I'd made a major mistake. I was grateful that she had recognised that it was a genuine error on my part and that I had not tried to claim for hours that I hadn't worked which would have been classed as fraud. This would have been a sackable offence.

I quickly generated a new timesheet and went to see my manager. He was okay about it but warned me to be very careful,

"They are very hot on things like this but I'm sure they are treating it as a simple error. It is your first timesheet after all. If you'd claimed for hours that you hadn't worked then believe me, it would be a lot more serious."

I took the 'telling-off' on the chin. I was so grateful to get this position that I didn't want anything to spoil it.

The administrator lady studied my new timesheet and invoice carefully,

"This looks correct."

"Thanks, and sorry for the last one."

"No problem. I'll ensure that this is processed."

"That's very kind of you."

I turned and left her office. I let out a huge sigh of relief as I walked back to my desk. I realised that I'd just had a very lucky escape.

***

There was some post waiting for me when I was back in

Scotland. They had sent me my company PAYE reference number along with a book of Giro payment slips. This meant that I was now in a position to set up my own payroll. This was a big step for me as it meant that I could now pay myself.

Early on Sunday morning I loaded the payroll software on to my personal computer from a 3.5-inch floppy disk. I entered in my new employer 'PAYE reference number' along with my company details. I then went on to enter my personal details which included my earnings from my previous employer which I obtained from my P45.

I knew that my contracting earnings were about four times what I'd previously been earning as an employee. This was going to put me into the higher tax bracket but we were in the last period of the current financial year so it was important that I used up my tax allowance that I had left before the new financial year started.

I played about with the numbers and once I was happy, I did a live 'payroll run'. This gave me the tax and NI I needed to pay to the Inland Revenue along with my net earnings for the month.

The problem I had was that as I hadn't been paid for the work I'd done; I didn't have any money in my new business account.

It was important that I didn't send my tax and NI in late so I wrote a cheque from my personal bank account, filled in the Giro payment slip and asked Jayne to pay it in at the bank when she got a moment.

I was surprised how easy it was. I knew that I needed to back everything up to a floppy disk but to be sure I also printed out a paper copy and put it in my bag to take back to Munich.

Jayne was a little annoyed that I was doing this on a weekend that I was at home but I needed to do it on my own computer. I also realised that as I was now self-employed, I had no choice but to spend my spare time doing these important business tasks.

***

It was clear to me that Jayne was getting a little frustrated living alone with George to look after so when I was back in Munich, I decided to ask Ron for a favour.

"What do you think about me bringing my wife Jayne and our young son over for a couple of weeks?"

"I don't have a problem with that but you won't all fit in your room so we will have to swap for the time you are here."

"Are you sure?"

"Of course, I go back at weekends so it's not a problem."

"Thanks, very much. I'll let her know."

This was really generous of him and I really appreciated it. The next day I phoned Jayne and told her that it was okay for her to visit. She was delighted and promptly booked some flights.

***

The IT project I was working on was still in the 'scoping phase' so there were lots of meetings where different ideas were thrown around. The team consisted of a small group of very experienced IT people and I found it all very interesting. My experience of working for the same company was really useful as I was able to contribution to the discussions.

It was a different type of work for me and I found it a little strange. I was used to working in the 'real world' where I was expected to fix a program because there was a 'panic on' because something wasn't working and this was affecting 'the business'.

I often felt as if I hadn't done a proper day's work but I knew that when we came to write the software this was going to change.

***

I enjoyed my weekend at home in Scotland and what made it a little extra special was that I didn't have to travel back to Munich alone as Jayne and George were going to be flying back with me.

Jayne had booked the flights and had managed to get a 'good deal' but this time we were going to fly via Amsterdam's Schiphol airport. This meant using two different airlines but they had an agreement so the bags would automatically be transferred between the planes.

I was a little excited about flying on a British Aerospace 146 for the first time. I'd heard a lot about this aircraft and knew that it was often referred to as 'the whisper jet'. When we boarded, I could see that it was a small but very well-designed aircraft.

"Do we get a meal on this plane?" said Jayne.

"I don't know, I assume so but I've not flown this route before so I don't know for certain."

The plane took off and once we'd gained a good altitude, I expected to be served a drink or something or eat, but I couldn't see the cabin crew preparing anything. This was a little frustrating as I was feeling rather hungry.

The plane's intercom came to life and an announcement was made,

"Would everyone please return to your seats as we are starting our descent."

I couldn't believe it; we'd hardly been in the air at all and now we were coming into land. I knew that these planes were good but blinking heck...

Jayne turned to me and said,

"That was quick, I can see now why we didn't get anything to eat or drink."

We taxied towards the stand and looking out of the window I could see a lot of helicopters but didn't think anything of it as I hadn't flown into Schiphol before. The intercom came to life again.

"Ladies and Gentlemen please remain seated whilst the aircraft is taxiing to the stand and welcome to Aberdeen."

Jayne and I both looked at each other and simultaneously said,

"ABERDEEN!"

"What are we doing in Aberdeen?"

"I don't know but I'm getting worried now."

"Do you think that we got on the wrong plane?"

"We can't have. I mean, we've booked through to Munich and you can't just walk onto any old plane."

Once the plane came to a halt, I watched some passengers get off and then asked an attendant,

"Excuse me; I assume that we are on the right plane to Amsterdam?"

"Yes Sir, Amsterdam is our next destination. This is just a stop-over."

"Thank you. I thought that we got to Amsterdam a bit quick."

She smiled at me and said,

"Just make yourself comfortable, we will be taking off very soon."

"Thank you."

I turned to Jayne,

"Phew, I was getting worried then."

"So was I."

"I can't believe that no-one said anything when we booked in."

"Now I know why there are so many helicopters. They are here to transport people to and from the oil rigs."

It wasn't long before we were airborne again and as soon as we were at cruising altitude, we were served a very nice meal.

***

Walking around Schiphol we stumbled upon a booth that sold diamonds. Jayne was immediately interested and started to ask lots of questions to the young man behind the counter. I was completely out of my depth when it came to talking about diamonds, it was something that didn't interest me in the slightest but I could see that Jayne found it all fascinating.

Jayne was wearing a solitaire diamond ring that had been specially made by her Grandfather for her Grandmother. She slipped it off and gave it to the man for his opinion.

Much to Jayne's delight he seemed impressed with the diamond but he didn't give an estimate of its value which would have been interesting although I knew that Jayne would never sell it. However, he was a skilled salesman and before I knew it Jayne was looking at diamond earrings that he thought would complement her beautiful ring.

I could see where this was heading but I just went along with it. In the end Jayne settled on a pair of earrings that she liked. The price didn't seem that expensive so I agreed that she could have them. She was obviously delighted as we walked to the gate for our flight to Munich. I was a little bewildered that we'd made such a large 'out of the blue' purchase but she was happy and that's what really mattered.

When I thought about what we'd been through recently I felt that Jayne deserved a treat. I was happy that she was happy but I made a 'mental note' to myself that next time we flew to Munich I would book the flights and ensure that we would transfer planes at either Manchester or Birmingham.

***

CHAPTER 4:

EASTER.

I struck up a conversation with the man who was sitting next to me on the plane. He was middle-aged American and slightly overweight. He came across as extremely well educated and my first impression was that he was probably an executive at one of the many top IT companies that reside in Munich but this turned out not to be the case.

The first thig that intrigued me was that a young man who was seated a few rows ahead of us kept turning to look at him. I got the impression that he was checking to see that he was okay. Originally, I thought that he was his minder but he didn't look physically strong enough.

I was surprised when he said that he was serving in the United Stated Army. I told him that I was in the British Army but he didn't seem very impressed. The conversation was very flat and there clearly was no special relationship developing between us.

It was a surreal situation but I just had to ask,

"So, what are you going to be doing in Munich?"

"We are not going to Munich; we are changing planes there and are heading to Yugoslavia."

I knew that there was a bit of conflict going on there and that the Americans were involved but I didn't know that much about it. He turned to me and said in a very 'matter of fact' manner,

"The thing is that they are behaving as if they are ten feet tall."

He spoke slowly and clearly and there was a high degree of confidence in his voice. I realised that this chap was used to getting his own way and I didn't know what to say as he continued,

"But they aren't ten feet tall."

That was just about the end of our conversation but he'd said enough to let me know that he was a hard man and probably very senior in the most powerful Army in the world.

I've thought about that short conversation a lot over the years. It reflected the confidence that Americans have. 'Bold as brass' as the saying goes. In my experience I'd never heard a British Army Officer speak like that.

My understanding was that he was saying that they aren't ten feet tall but we are. What it must be like to be a superpower?

I will always believe that the British Army is the best in the world but unfortunately, we are no longer a superpower. Nowadays you could nearly fit our entire regular Army inside Wembley football stadium.

***

We caught the S-Bahn from the airport to Daglfing station and walking towards the apartment we passed the local supermarket where I turned to Jayne and said,

"That's where I bought the beer from."

"Okay. As soon as we are organised, I'll come back with George and get some provisions."

"Fine."

Ron and I had already swapped rooms in anticipation for Jayne's arrival. His room had a double bed and we'd bought a fold-up carrycot for George to sleep in. Once Jayne knew where everything was in the apartment, I left her to settle in and walked to the office.

It was a nice feeling walking back to the apartment a few hours later knowing that my family were there waiting for me. The first thing I noticed when I opened the door was the smell which told me that Jayne has obviously sussed out how the cooker worked.

I was really looking forward to a family meal and I shouted out,

"Hello darling, I'm home."

"Good, dinner's nearly ready."

"Excellent, it smells fantastic."

I went over to George who gave me a big smile as I picked him up. I carried him around whilst chatting to Jayne. We sat down and ate a nice meal. Ron joined us later but retired to his room leaving us to it.

It was great being a family again and I appreciated the simple things in life more that I normally would.

On Saturday morning we decided to go into the centre of Munich and see the sights. It was sunny and there were a lot of people about but there was still a bit of a winter chill in the air. We spent some time at the beautiful Marienplatz which had a very Germanic feel about it due to the beautiful town hall which was on the northern side of the open square.

We were lucky enough to witness the glockenspiel chime in the hour which was just enchanting. Looking around we went into a restaurant that had a completely open frontage which meant that although we were inside, it felt like we were outside. We ordered two 'Zigeuner schnitzels mit pommes' ('Gypsy' pork schnitzel with a spicy tomato and mushroom sauce with chips).

It was a bit expensive but we were in the city centre and thought that we deserved a treat. Looking out through the huge opening I couldn't understand where the wall had gone. It hadn't been 'folded back' and there didn't seem to be any indication that it was stored somewhere.

George was getting a little restless so I manoeuvred his buggy in to a better position so we could give him something to eat. The wheel of his buggy got stuck so I looked down to see what was causing the problem and the I realised what it was.

The missing wall had been lowered down so that it was below ground level and completely out of the way. There must have been some mechanism that made this happen which was a really clever bit of engineering. I was impressed with this and thought it was a brilliant idea. I wondered if the architect had been influenced by 'Tracy Island'; the home of the Thunderbirds.

**

We walked about a bit more and then we came across a café that had a small seating area outside so we decided to have a coffee. We sat outside with our coats on but George became a bit restless so I let him out of his buggy and held his hand tightly as we walked around a small pedestrian area.

George was straining my arm trying to get away from me but I wouldn't let him go. Jayne was watching us as we walked towards her and as we got nearer to her, I released my grip. He took a few steps unaided before Jayne grabbed him under his arms. I couldn't believe it; George had just walked unaided for the first time in his life and I was there to see it.

**

The Easter weekend was approaching and Jayne and I spent some time discussing what we wanted to do. It was an opportunity to see a bit more of the countryside so in the end we decided to hire a car.

Looking at the map we both agreed that we would like to visit the Austrian city of Salzburg. We hadn't been there before and as it was only 90 miles or so from Munich, we thought it would be an easy enough journey, especially as there was a good autobahn that went straight there.

We set off on the Saturday morning; there wasn't much traffic on the road and we seemed to get there in no time. I drove around and found a parking space on the side of the road which didn't seem to have any restrictions.

We made our way towards the centre. Jayne was pushing George in his buggy and I carried the bags. Looking around we found a small guesthouse and managed to get a room for one night. This was perfect for us and after we'd settled in, we went out to explore the city.

Mozart was born in Salzburg and his presence seemed to permeate to this day. The beautiful architecture seemed to reflect a lovely romantic bygone era.

The atmosphere of the city was so absorbing that we felt like we had gone back in time two hundred years and half expected to see Mozart come walking around the corner whistling a new composition of his. It was enchanting.

We went into a traditional restaurant for dinner which I'm sure had 'Mozart' in its name and settled down to some traditional Germanic style food (Schnitzel again). George was sat in his high chair and Jayne fed him some food that she had prepared earlier. In the middle of the table was a little bowl that contained some small chocolate eggs (well it was Easter). This was a nice touch and added to the atmosphere.

The waitress was a middle-aged woman who took a real liking to George and kept making a fuss of him. This was very nice but George was a little restless after the long journey and wasn't on his best behaviour.

Jayne and I ordered some coffees and just wanted to relax but somehow George managed to grab one of the small chocolate eggs and put it straight into his mouth. I couldn't believe it and looked at him for a moment not knowing what to do.

Jayne screamed at me,

"Get it out of his mouth!"

George's face was 'screwed up', he obviously didn't like the taste of the egg which was understandable as it still had its foil wrapping on it. I put my finger into his mouth and eventually managed to get the soggy chocolatey foil mess out.

I thought that that would be the end of the matter and that Jayne and I could enjoy our coffees but although George didn't like the foil, he obviously liked the chocolate and kept wriggling as he tried to get out of his high-chair to grab another egg.

The waitress came over and Jayne gave her the small bowl of eggs so that she could take them away but a moment later the waitress returned with an unwrapped chocolate egg and popped it straight into George's mouth.

Jayne and I were mortified. We had never given George chocolate before and couldn't believe that a stranger had done so without our permission. We knew that she was being nice but we weren't happy about at all.

I thought about putting my fingers back into George's mouth but decided against it. There was no foil on it this time so George was able to chew it without any problems. We both just watched him closely to make sure that he didn't choke. George of course loved the chocolate and wanted some more but we quickly finished our coffees and left.

Jayne was fuming,

"How dare she do that?"

"I know, I was really shocked."

"George is our child and we decide what he eats."

"I guess she thought she was being nice."

"But what if he had an allergy or something?"

"That's what worried me, he hasn't had chocolate before."

We both felt that the waitress had over-stepped the mark and that in some way our position as parents had been violated. We couldn't undo what had just happened but we both intended to be more vigilant in future. George wasn't bothered at all and probably enjoyed the fuss as much as he enjoyed the chocolate.

***

We only stayed one night in Salzburg and the next day we made our way back to Munich. Later in the evening when we were back in the apartment we sat down and had a beer. George was asleep and we sat on the sofa reflecting on our nice little trip.

"Who'd have thought a year ago that we would be spending Easter in Munich?"

"I know, you couldn't make it up, could you?"

"We'd just got the house how we wanted it in Scotland and then George arrived."

"Yes, we spent all that time and energy moving up there and once we had everything sorted, they closed the factory and made me redundant."

"That really wasn't fair was it?"

"No. Unfortunately companies don't care about being fair."

"But at least you managed to get some work over here."

"Yes, it was a strange twist of fate but it will keep us going for a bit."

"How long do you think you'll be here?"

"It depends on how long the project will take. It hasn't really got going yet. We are still throwing ideas around."

"It makes it difficult to plan things."

"I know but its work and I'm hoping I can be here as long as I can. Its good money and we should have a nice deposit sitting in the bank when we eventually decide to buy another house."

"It's a shame that the house in Scotland isn't selling."

"I know, I can't believe that."

"It's just a bit of a stagnant market at the moment."

"When I think of all the hassle that we went through moving up there and now we can't sell the house to move back home."

"I'm sure it will sell eventually."

"Let's hope so."

***

There was a place to the north west of Munich that I thought was worth a visit. It probably wasn't a very good destination for a family day-out but it was an important place that had intrigued me for years. We had nothing else to do and we still wanted to make some use of the hire-car so we decided to go.

It didn't take long to drive the 18 miles or so to a small town to the north west of Munich. Looking around it looked extremely attractive and well kept. It appeared to be a very affluent area which reminded me of 'leafy suburbia'.

There was a small carpark near our destination. It was very quiet and there were not many people about as we put George in his buggy. I was surprised how near to Munich it was. I always imagined these places to be extremely remote and tucked away but this was not the case.

I've spent a lot of my life in military institutions and initially I got the same 'vibe' as we approached the camp. I stopped pushing the buggy for a moment and looked at it. It did indeed look a normal old 'war time' military institution but there was nothing normal about this place. I was looking at Dachau Nazi concentration camp.

When we got to the entrance the assistant was not happy that we had a young child with us and at one point I thought that they were not going to let us in. I realised that there were strict age guidelines which upon reflection made very good sense. It was only because George was so young that they relented and let us in.

We walked into the open space I soon realised that this was a sterile, lifeless and eerie place. I'd read an account somewhere where it was said that the birds don't sing in such places but this was not the case. However, it was extremely quiet.

There were only a handful of other visitors walking around the main compound so it felt like we had the whole place to ourselves. There wasn't much left of the internal accommodation buildings, in fact there was only one there and my understanding was that it had been reconstructed (there are two there now).

There was a large building in the compound which looked to me like it could have been the camp headquarters (according to the map it was the maintenance building). This contained a permanent exhibition which had lots of historical information, artefacts and photographs.

We went over to the accommodation building and looked in through the windows. It was a little disappointing that we weren't allowed inside but I knew what it would have been like as I'd see many pictures and films on the subject.

You could clearly see where all the other accommodation buildings had been as they had left the layout intact. I counted two rows of seventeen. That's thirty-four buildings all crammed with people, it must have been mayhem.

We walked along and tried to imagine what it would have been like when it was full of people. The camp had clearly been very well designed.

There were some religious memorials at the far end but as we approached, we turned to the left towards the 'ovens'. The thought of what it must have been like was just horrible. I felt sure that the 'inmates' would have known what was going on and the odds of them surviving would have been extremely small. The people who carried out those atrocities must have completely 'switched-off' their emotions.

I really felt it was important to go and visit a place like Dachau; it was a good place to reflect and digest what can go wrong in our world. The total lack of humanity was appalling. To conceive an idea like that was unbelievable but to actually carry it out in a systematic and cold way was difficult to comprehend.

Jayne and I had been blessed with a healthy young son and our lives were focused on his safety and his needs. This place was all about the destruction of life. It was extremely hard to comprehend and shows what can happen when people in power go too far.

We left the camp feeling in a very sombre mood. Making our way to the car as a family I just felt so lucky and relieved that I hadn't experienced what the 'inmates' of

Dachau had gone through. Visiting a place that that was extremely important and I really appreciated the fact that we could just walk away from it and get on with our lives.

***

My main skillset at work was working on the main business computer system. The hardware was a Hewlett Packard HP3000. Technically it was a 'super minicomputer' but as it was a centralised system it could have been thought of as a mainframe.

I'd spent sometime during my redundancy period teaching myself some new Personal Computer skills or to be more specific the popular business software that runs on most PC's. I thought that I had done very well but it soon became clear that I was nowhere near the level that some of the younger members of the team were.

The team consisted of a few university students who were spending a 'placement year' in Munich gaining some valuable work experience. They were a really good bunch and helped out with all sorts of tasks.

They didn't have any experience of the HP3000 computer system and didn't see it as 'the future' so they weren't bothered about learning this technology. However, they were very experienced in using the more modern PC software and this is where they spent a lot of their time developing their skills even more.

One chap in particular picked up on my lack of Personal Computer skills. I thought I was doing okay but he was a little bewildered at my lack of knowledge considering that I was a highly paid IT contractor.

I was okay with a bit of teasing especially as he had saved me a lot of time by answering some of my very basic questions but one day, he turned to me and said,

"The problem with you Harry, is that you are just an old fashioned 'Green Screener'".

The PC's we used were nice and modern compared with the main IT system. It was only a few years previously that you connected to the HP3000 using a VDU (Visual Display Unit) which were also known as 'dumb terminals'.

Some special software had been installed on the PC's which gave them the capability to act as a computer terminal linked to the main system. This was really useful but you could easily see the differences in two technologies on the screen.

Unfortunately, this gave some credence to my new nickname which was becoming popular with the younger generation of IT professionals. In his eyes I would will always be known as,

"A Green Screener".

***

It was Saturday morning and looking out of the apartment window I could see that it was going to be a really good day. The sun was shining and although I thought it would still be a bit chilly, I felt that it was definitely a day to be outside.

Munich had hosted the 1972 Olympic games and I'd seen the famous 'spider web' stadium on TV many times before. Now it was the home ground of the famous Bayern Munich football team but it still had its running track.

We travelled on the S-Bahn across Munich to the Olympic Park and when we ventured out into the open, I was surprised how warm it was. I found it difficult to understand how quickly the weather had changed from being snowy to being 'spring like'.

The park was dominated by the famous Olympic Tower and we walked over to take a closer look. There were some fascinating photographs on display of it being built. The pictures that impressed me the most were not the ones of the tower but the ones that showed its foundations; they were just so deep and so solid. Building the tower and the Olympic park must have been an enormous project.

Initially I thought that we would go up the tower but Jayne didn't like heights. I wasn't sure if George or buggies would be allowed and I didn't really want to go up alone so we carried on with our walk.

The architecture of the various arenas was really interesting, there was probably nothing like it anywhere else in the world and it was good to see that it was still being used. These were clearly world class facilities which had now become a fantastic legacy.

The main stadium was obviously the biggest landmark after the tower. I had a lot of respect for athletes at any level but to be that talented and dedicated to represent your country at the Olympics must be a tremendous feeling.

In the distance but not too far away stood an unusual looking office block, instead of being rectangular it appeared to consist of four vertical cylinders. It was silver and glistened in the sunlight. I looked at it for a while and thought that it wouldn't look out of place in outer-space as it wasn't dissimilar to a space station.

It was a while before I remembered what it was,

"That's BMW's headquarters."

"Is it?"

"Yes, apparently it has a museum attached to it."

"That's interesting."

"We could take a look if you like?"

"We can do that if you want although I'm not sure how long it will take to walk there."

"There's a bridge across the duel-carriageway. If we cross that then hopefully there will be some signs."

We headed off in a northerly direction and found the footbridge; we then followed some signs to the museum which was housed in its own building which didn't look unlike a breakfast bowl with a flat lid.

I often think of industry especially manufacturing as dirty and noisy but this area appeared to be more suited to the space age. To me, it was a fantastic showcase of German engineering and a statement of National identity.

The museum was pristine inside and I was immediately drawn to the early displays. My knowledge of BMW was extremely limited. I didn't know anything at all about its history and when I thought about the brand, I just thought of a range of powerful saloon cars designed to speed along the German Autobahns which don't have a speed limit.

The layout was circular and you went up a gentle slope in a clockwise direction. I looked with interest at the cars on display and then I came across a model that I could remember being on the road. It was called an 'Isetta' which was manufactured by BMW under license from the Italian company Iso. I was shocked to discover that it had BMW heritage as it was so tiny. To get in, you literally opened up the complete front of the car which was designed to be a door, it even had the steering wheel connected to it. This car is often known as the iconic 'Bubble Car' which was originally manufactured in the 1950's.

I was really enjoying my visit but unfortunately George decided to 'play up' a bit. He wasn't interested in cars or museums and to be fair to him it had been a long day. I really wanted to explore the museum a lot more we had no choice but to leave; such is the life of a dad.

***

A few days later, I left Jayne in the apartment and went into work early. George was still asleep and this gave Jayne some time to finish packing before having to deal with his needs. They were both flying back to the UK in the afternoon.

I walked around the rear of the apartment block and looked up to see Jayne on the balcony giving me a big wave. I waved back and blew her a kiss. It was a nice moment.

Just before lunch I left the office and started my twenty-minute walk back to the apartment. It had been a great couple of weeks. We'd been blessed with some good weather which had allowed us to get out and about.

Just being a young family again had been a pure joy. I'd got to know George a bit more and witnessed some of his development first-hand.

Life just seemed to not want us to be together. I was lucky that Jayne was a strong enough person to be able to cope but I knew that sometimes she found it difficult. We knew that things would get better once we sold the house in Scotland as this would allow us to relocate back home to England and be near our family and friends.

When I got back to the apartment and could see that everything was ready which didn't surprise me as Jayne was usually, very well organised. There was no point in hanging around so we made our way to the S-Bahn station for the direct train to the airport. We didn't say much as we sat on the train and I did my best to entertain George.

The airport was not as busy as it usually was when I travelled home on a Friday which was appreciated as we had a lot of luggage. We joined a small queue at the check-in desk and then made our way to departures where we said our goodbyes.

***

CHAPTER 5:

LEAVING SCOTLAND WITH A BANG.

The two weeks 'working away from home' became our new way of life. Work-life balance didn't exist for us but we just got on with it as best we could.

I was settling in really well and getting to know everyone. They were a really good bunch and everyone seemed to be willing to help each other out.

I wanted to make sure that I earnt as much money as I could while the work was available. The days became very long but nobody seemed to mind how many hours people put in.

Speaking to Jayne on the phone she said,

"Harry, you will be pleased to know that they have paid your first invoice."

"What! That's brilliant."

"They converted it into Sterling automatically as you can't have Deutschmarks in a UK GBP bank account. I think that they just used the exchange rate at the time."

"Wow, this is actually happening."

"It's taken two months but we are now making some money out of this."

"I'll now be able to pay myself."

"Don't forget all of your expenses. I bet you've spent an awful lot of money on flights and accommodation."

"True, I think that this payment will just about cover

everything I've spent so far but my second invoice is still outstanding so we should be in the 'black' next month."

"I thought you'd be pleased."

"Pleased, I'm 'over the moon'. That really is good news. Anyway, I best get on. Speak to you tomorrow."

"Okay, love you."

"Love you too."

I put the phone down very slowly. It was a seminal moment; after all the hassle we'd been through I was now 'up and running' as a contractor. It was a great feeling and it felt even better knowing that no 'agency' or 'consultancy' was making any money out of me this time.

***

The weekends when I was alone in Munich were the hardest thing to cope with. I just didn't know what to do with myself. I'd always filled my spare time with lots of things but here I was, in a foreign country with nothing to do.

Munich is the main city in Bavaria and has excellent communication links in the region. One Sunday afternoon I was walking through the main railway station and I saw someone coming out of a shop carrying an English newspaper.

I went in and had a look around and it didn't take me long to find several stacks of English Sunday newspapers. To me this was a brilliant find and I promptly picked up the biggest one that contained lots of different segments.

It turned out to be a little expensive at 8DM but I always loved reading the Sunday papers. I walked around and found a quiet bar that had a few tables outside so I sat down and ordered a beer.

The weather was lovely and I sat there slowing drinking my beer reading the paper. I lost myself in my reading and ended up sitting there for a couple of hours before going to get something to eat. I then made my way back to the apartment where I promptly fell asleep on the sofa.

***

One Saturday evening Jayne and I were sitting in the Strathallen Pub having a drink. It was very quiet and as we sat their together, I turned to her and said,

"I'm going to miss this place."

"Yes, it was quite a find."

"I don't think we will ever be this lucky again."

"I know what you mean, it's been a great experience but at least we will have some really good memories."

"Yes, it's been quite an adventure. It's just a shame that it ended so quickly."

"There are no guarantees in this life, we made a choice and it's a real shame that it didn't work out."

"I guess we'll always visit here again, it will never leave us."

"Once we sell the house it will all be over. There will be no reason for us to come back here."

"I'm sure we will be back, even if it's only for a holiday."

"Anyway, changing the subject; now that you have been paid and hopefully you will be offered an extension to your contract, we need to make a decision. What are we going to do?"

"What are your thoughts?"

"Well, the way I see it, we have two choices. We can carry on as we are with you commuting back every other weekend or I can move to Munich."

"What about the house?"

"We are going to leave at some point, so I think that we should put all of our stuff in storage."

"And leave the house empty?"

"Yes."

"Wow, that's a big decision."

"We will have to give the keys to our estate agent and just hope that they can sell it."

"The trouble is that any potential buyer will know that we are desperate to sell and we won't get a decent price."

"But what else can we do? We can't leave all of our belongings there with no one to look after them."

"Okay, I agree that we can't go on living like this. Can you make some enquiries about removal companies and storage?"

"Yes, but I think I would prefer our belongings to be stored 'down south' rather than up here."

"Okay, if that's what you want. I still can't believe that we are having this conversation, it only eighteen months ago that we moved up here."

"Yes, and your company paid for the move. Now we've got to pay out of our own pocket to move back home."

"Perhaps we should have put a clause in my employment contract that if they made me redundant then they would pay for me to relocate back home."

"I don't think that they would have agreed to that."

"True, but it makes you think. Wasn't there a politician who said that you need to go on your bike to work? Well we did that and look what happened."

"There's no point in getting wound up about it now. It is what it is and at least you are in work."

"That's true. Do you know what? If this is the end of this phase in our lives then I think that we should mark the occasion somehow."

"I don't think another party is appropriate, it's not really a celebration."

"I'll tell you what, I'll get the drinks in and we will have a think about it."

I went over to the bar and felt pleased that we'd made a decision. I was a little concerned about leaving the house empty but it seemed the best thing to do, given our circumstances.

I was disappointed that there weren't any of our friends in the pub but at least that meant that we could have a chat about things. I returned to our table with the drinks and said,

"Any ideas?"

"I do actually. I think that it's time to treat ourselves."

***

I arrived in the office one Friday morning happy that I was flying home in the afternoon. I had my large hold-all bag with me which mostly contained my laundry.

There was a young member of our team called Callum, he was from the midlands and was a real 'techie'. He looked at me and said,

"Are you off home for the weekend Harry?"

"Yes," I replied.

"I take it you are here next weekend then?"

"Yes, unfortunately."

"Well, how would you like to have my hire-car for the weekend that you are here? I'm going back to the UK so you can borrow it if you like."

"What about insurance and all that?"

"I'll phone them but I think it will be okay as long as you have a full UK license."

"I've got more than that, I've got an HGV license or LGV as it is now called."

"Well that should be okay then."

He didn't comment on my HGV and I guess he assumed that I got this during my time in the Army which was correct.

On the flight to Manchester I thought about the next weekend. It would be great to have a car but I wasn't sure where I would drive it. Public transport was fantastic so there was no point going anywhere in the city.

Looking out of the plane window the idea came to me that it would be good to go camping. The Alps were only an hour's drive away from Munich and I thought that there must be plenty of campsites there, all I needed to do over the weekend was to grab my hike tent, sleeping bag and a few camping bits and I would be set.

Jayne didn't seem bothered that I was planning a camping weekend without her.

"You're there anyway so you may as well see a bit of the country."

"Are you sure you don't mind?"

"No, if Callum is lending you his car it makes sense to use it."

"Okay, but I wanted to clear it with you first."

"No problem, go and make the most of it."

***

The next weekend Callum gave me the keys to his car and helped me carry my bags that contained my camping equipment down to the underground carpark. It was a small Opel Corsa which was ideal for me.

I made up some sandwiches at lunchtime which I thought I would have for my dinner as I didn't know where I was going to end up staying.

I adjusted the car seat and mirrors and gingerly drove up the ramp and out of the carpark. It wasn't long before I was slowly driving down the autobahn in a southerly direction. I took a chance and turned off and headed towards the mountains that I could see in the distance.

It was getting late but I was confident that I would find somewhere to stay but as I drove along, I didn't see any camping signs.

I kept on driving from place to place and eventually came to a small town called Starnberg. I noticed a camping sign as I was driving through so I turned left and followed a road that took me out of the town and around a large lake to a youth hostel that had a small area that was being used as a campsite.

I registered and quickly put up my tent which was in a really nice spot not too far from the lake's edge. There were no facilities such as a clubhouse so I started to walk back along the road towards the town. It was further than I would have liked and I munched on my sandwiches as I walked along.

An old car passed me and stopped and as I walked up to it a middle-aged woman asked,

"Do you want a lift?"

I looked at her and realised that she had been at the campsite.

"Yes please. I'm just going into town for a beer."

"So are we, hop in."

There were three other people in the car so I squashed into the back and was grateful that the two occupants didn't cause too much fuss as they shuffled along the seat. They carried on talking in German and didn't pay much attention to me. I was grateful for the lift but wished that my German was a better so I could understand what they were talking about.

We arrived at a bar and we all went in. I offered to buy my new friends a drink but they were meeting some other people so I left them to it and just ordered a single beer for myself.

I walked over to a small empty table and sat down. I found myself thinking,

"What the hell am I doing here?"

I didn't know what to expect when I set off only a couple of hours earlier but at least I'd managed to find somewhere to pitch my tent. I thought that there would be lots of campsites.

I ordered another beer and could see the people I shared a lift with were enjoying themselves at the other end of the bar. I finished my beer and went over to them and indicated that I was leaving. The driver nodded to me and then carried on talking to her companions.

It was a long walk back in the dark but I eventually made it and was soon in my sleeping bag. One good thing about the walk was that I had several toilet breaks so I knew that I wouldn't have to get up in the night which I always found a problem when I was tucked up in my sleeping bag.

*

The next morning, I climbed out of my tent and was please that it looked like it was going to be a beautiful day. I made up some cereal for my breakfast which was followed by a mug of hot tea. I fancied doing some hiking but I didn't have a map so in the end I decided to walk around the lake.

Looking at the lake I realised that it was just too big to

walk around so in the end I walked back into town. I went into the railway station and it became clear to me that I wasn't very far from Munich. It would have been quicker and a lot easier if I'd just caught a train.

There wasn't much to see and there weren't many people about so I soon ended up in the same bar that I'd been in the night before. I ordered a zigeuner schnitzel mit pommes accompanied by the obligatory Helles (beer). I then thought that perhaps the beer was a mistake as I could have used the car to explore the area a bit more.

I enjoyed my lunch and then headed back to my tent. I 'brewed-up' and had an early night.

The next morning, I packed everything up straight away and drove back to Munich. It had been good to do a bit more exploring but my mistake was that I hadn't planned it very well.

It would also have been a lot better if I'd been able to share the experience with Jayne but I knew that there was no way that she would go camping with me again, especially as we now had a toddler to look after.

***

I was pleased to be back in Scotland for the weekend as I knew it was going to be really special. We'd arranged for both Jaynes and my parents to visit us but rather than travel up by train we'd treated them to flights from Birmingham to Edinburgh.

I really wanted to pick them up from the airport, but Jayne insisted that she wanted to do it, so I stayed at home and looked after George.

It was lovely to see them when they walked into the house. They had really enjoyed their flights and looked like real 'jet setters' with their luggage.

My mum's name was Anna and I'm pretty sure that it was the first time that she had ever been on a plane; I think that my dad had only been on one when he did his National Service when he served in the RAF.

They didn't know what we had planned which was

perhaps a little unsettling for them but we wanted it to be a surprise. They had made a few guesses and my mum said that she thought that she was going hot-air ballooning. I don't know where that idea came from, but their guesses made it all the more fun.

Jayne had arranged for our friend Elspeth to do everyone's hair on the Saturday morning. My mum thought it was a waste of money as she still thought that we were going to send her up in a balloon.

We had spoken to Jamie who I'd worked with at the factory about our plans a few weeks earlier. I told him that we needed a posh car and asked if he could recommend anyone. He phoned me back later and said that he'd sorted everything out and that his dad had offered to drive our parents.

This was just fantastic and to top it all off Jamie offered to drive Jayne and me in his car. There was a real sense that our friends wanted to get involved in our 'little plot' which just added to the excitement.

Everyone looked lovely in their 'glad rags' and there was a real sense of anticipation in the air as we waited for the cars to arrive. Jayne and I went out of our house and stood by the road. The weather wasn't very good, but at least it wasn't raining.

A really nice silver Mercedes slowly came down our street and stopped outside our house. I thought that this was a mistake and then out stepped Jamie's dad who was immaculately dressed in his tartan kilt. Jayne and I couldn't believe what we were looking at, it was just perfect.

Jamie then turned up in his own car and parked behind his dad. The two drivers then came into our house where we introduced them to our parents. We chatted for a while before we all went outside and settled our parents into the nice posh Mercedes. Jayne and I watched them drive off and then got into Jamie's car and headed after them.

Jamie's car was bright red and really sporty, but he drove very sedately following his dad. I thought about our parents in the car in front. They weren't used to being treated like royalty but that was the point. It was time to give something back.

Unfortunately, it started to rain so we missed some beautiful views. Our parents still didn't know where they were going and when the Mercedes turned into the entrance to a Scottish country estate Jamie's dad stopped the car for a few seconds near the entrance sign to give his passengers a chance to read it, but due to the poor weather none of them noticed it.

Gleneagles hotel is an impressive building set in beautiful grounds, but I wouldn't say that it was particularly attractive. From the outside it reminded me of a 'Sandhurst' barrack block that I'd stayed in whilst serving in the Army at Catterick garrison.

The Mercedes came to a gentle stop at the entrance to the hotel. It was still raining quite hard, so Jamie's dad got out of his driver's seat and made his way to the back of the car where he opened the boot; at the same time Jayne's mum Lilly opened the rear passenger door, swung her legs round, hitched her dress up and made a dash towards the hotel entrance as fast as she could.

She didn't realise that at the time she did this, Jamie's dad was right behind her and had opened an umbrella as he was just about to escort her up the steps. Jayne screamed at her,

"Wait a minute, Mum!" but to no avail as she was half way up the steps before she realised what was happening and then it was too late; the moment had passed.

Jamie's dad stood there in the rain looking a bit bewildered but his gallantry wasn't wasted as my mum got out of the car very graciously and let him escort her up the steps in a very dignified manner. She reminded us of the Queen mother which became her 'nickname' for the evening.

*

Our two dads joined us and we decided to go into the bar area for a drink before going into the restaurant. I let them go before me and then I went back out of the hotel and thanked Jamie and his dad for their kind efforts.

"Would you like to come in for a drink?"

They looked at each other for a second and then Jamie's dad replied,

"That would be very nice thanks. We'll park the cars in the carpark and will be there in a moment."

I dashed back into the hotel before I got too wet and joined my family.

It was extremely busy but we managed to find an area where we could all sit down together. The two drivers managed to find us so I made my way to the bar and bought them two non-alcoholic drinks.

It was lovely sitting there, everyone was 'dressed up' and in good spirits. We all sat there chatting away like it was an everyday occurrence.

Some olives were deposited on the table and my mother promptly tried one. Once she was finished Jayne turned to her and said,

"Well Anna, you can now say that you've eaten at Gleneagles."

"Yes, indeed."

Jayne was being a little cheeky implying that the olives were all that we were going to get to eat but my mother was just going along with things and didn't react at all.

*

We finished our drinks and said farewell to our two fantastic drivers. They had really got into the spirit of what we were trying to do and added a unique Scottish touch that made it all the more special.

*

It was lovely going into the beautiful dining room. It just oozed class and luxury. We were shown to our table which was near a pianist who was in full flow on a lovely grand piano. The music helped create a lovely ambiance and we just knew that we were in for a real treat.

*

Once we had completed our first course my Dad turned around and said,

"Did you know that this hotel was once owned by British Rail?"

I looked at him dumbfounded; I knew that he worked on the railways but didn't expect him to come out with that remark.

"No, I didn't know that. I knew that the original rail companies built some fantastic hotels near the London terminals but I didn't know that Gleneagles was originally a railway hotel."

"Yes, I guess they thought that if they built a new country hotel near the railway line it would attract lots of visitors which would use the railway."

"That makes sense, I assume that they thought that one business would complement the other. It's a shame it's not owned by British Rail now or you might have been able to get us a staff discount!"

***

Jayne and I were talking to each other when we suddenly heard a distinctive 'clunk' that came from our table.

Quick as a flash Lilly turned to us and said,

"Oh, my God! Your dad's false teeth have just fallen into his teacup."

"You're joking!"

We both turned and stared at Oscar's cup where we could see that something was floating in it.

The waiter who was stood next to Oscar promptly picked up his cup and saucer and went off with it without saying a word.

"Where's he going with Dad's teeth?" screamed Jayne.

I couldn't figure out what was going on and looking at Oscar it looked like he didn't have a clue either. He then said,

"All I wanted was my tea topping up."

"Mum said that your teeth fell into the cup."

"No, it was the teapot lid as he was pouring it."

We all looked at Lilly and Jayne said,

"Mum you got me going there."

"Sorry, I couldn't resist it, but it is the sort of thing that your dad would do."

The waiter promptly returned with a clean cup and saucer for Oscar. He then poured in some milk followed by some freshly brewed tea.

"There you are Sir."

Oscar was happy now that he had a fresh cup of tea and we were all pleased that he hadn't disgraced our family in such a posh place.

*

After the meal we went through to a different room where a band was playing. We found ourselves somewhere to sit but soon ended up on the dance floor.

The band were really good and when they finished a DJ continued to keep things going until 2am. We were all extremely tired when our taxis turned up to take us home.

I must admit that I was a little envious of the other patrons who were staying the night. It would have been lovely for us to do the same but we needed to get back to look after George first thing in the morning and with six of us staying it would have been very expensive.

***

I sat in my seat on the plane to Munich with my Scotch and dry ginger reflecting on the lovely weekend I'd just had. Everyone had really enjoyed themselves; it had been well worth the hassle and expense of organising it (to be fair Jayne had done all the work).

We'd achieved our objective of leaving Scotland on a positive note. It had been a challenging time but a great experience. In two weeks, a truck will arrive at our house where a small team will pack up all of our possessions. They will then drive down to England and place everything in storage where it will remain for the foreseeable future.

It was really nice to have been in a position to be able to treat our parents; after all they had given us so much over the years. I was grateful that they had taken the effort to travel up to see us and for the lovely support we had from our friends, especially the drivers. The memory of that weekend has stayed with me ever since and I know that it will never leave me.

Life's journey is finite and has its 'ups and downs'. Reflecting on the 'good times' can often help you get through the 'hard times'. This was a really 'good time' and when Jayne and I look back on it now there is no doubt that 'doing something nice' for our parents when we could has helped us cope with life's inevitable conclusion.

No regrets.

***

CHAPTER 6:

FAMILY LIFE AGAIN.

We all piled into a German BrauHaus after work one day; everyone was in good spirits as we all tucked into our dinners. After a 'few beers' had been consumed the singing started.

I joined in the chorus of a few songs but again I found myself cursing that I didn't have a party piece that I could perform for everyone. It was then that I remembered a campfire song that we used to sing when I was in the Scouts, so I gave it a blast.

"On top of spaghetti, all covered in cheese, I lost my poor meatball when somebody sneezed..."

Fortunately, some of the team knew it and joined in. It wasn't a match for the songs that had been sung previously but at least I had a go.

A bit later, another tune popped into my head. I'd seen this performed brilliantly by some RAF chaps when I was in the Army stationed at RAF Wildenrath. It always got everyone going.

There was a pause in proceedings so I slowly stood up. Everyone was looking at me as I lifted my arms out in front of me and made a two nice 'O' shapes with each of my hands by touching my thumb and index finger together. I then twisted my hands so that my palms were facing me. I placed my hands against my head so that my eyes were looking through the circles. This was intended to represent a silly looking pair of flying goggles.

I then stood up and raised my elbows to the ceiling and started to sing.

"Naah Nah Nah... Naah Nana Nah Nah."

I then turned my body and tilted my elbows to make out that I was an aeroplane and that my elbows were my wings. The tune was known by all of the British members of the team as it was the music of the famous 'Dambusters' movie.

This was a true World War II story where a Squadron of RAF Lancaster Bombers destroyed several German dams by using the infamous 'bouncing bomb'.

I expected everyone to join in but that didn't happen, so I just carried on until the end. When I was finished, I lowered my arms to see that everyone was just staring at me open mouthed and this included some of the German diners.

It then hit me that this was not the NAAFI (servicemen's club) and these were civvies who hadn't experienced anything like that before.

I sat down quickly and thankfully someone else started singing which covered up my embarrassment. I didn't know it then but I'd earned myself a new nickname which was kept secret from me for a while, which was 'bomber'. I'm still referred to by this name today by the people who were there.

***

One evening whilst Ron and I were sitting down in the living room watching a video the doorbell rang. I went to see who it was and found myself looking at an elderly lady and a younger companion. The elderly lady looked me directly in the eye and said in English,

"Good evening, I've come to view the apartment."

"Err…"

I hesitated a little and didn't know what to say but fortunately Ron appeared behind me.

"Ah yes, I was told you were going to visit us today.

Please come in."

I was a little dismayed that I didn't know what was going on but I retreated into the hallway so that they could come in.

Ron said,

"Please do whatever you want to do. We'll leave you to it and if you need anything then just ask."

I noticed that the younger lady had a tape measure, a notebook and a pencil with her. She didn't appear to be able speak any English but immediately set to work measuring the rooms, windows and the cupboards.

The elderly lady walked around looking at all the rooms. It took a moment for me to realise it, but soon became clear to me that the lady was really upset. I got the impression that she was trying to put a brave face on things and I wondered what was going on.

It turned out that she had been living not very far from where we were in a large beautiful house but unfortunately, she had recently lost her husband and could no longer afford to live there.

She was a friend of our landlord and he had agreed to transfer the lease of the apartment over to her. I wasn't very knowledgeable of how the rental system worked in Germany but reading between the lines I sensed that she felt lucky that she had this option.

I found it a little heart-breaking to watch. Her world was imploding and she was of an age that meant that there was nothing she could do about it.

Her English was impeccable, she was obviously well educated and I listened intently as she told her story.

The ladies companion worked her way methodically through each room taking all the measurements that were required.

Once they had obtained all the information that they wanted. I showed them to the door but I didn't know what to say so I just wished her well with her move and hoped that she would be happy with the apartment.

*

That encounter had a big effect on me and still does. I really felt for her but it came down to the difference between renting and buying. I was only too aware that buying a property isn't without its drawbacks, especially when you consider that we'd been trying to sell a property for nearly a year without any luck.

It however, reaffirmed my ambition to own my own home outright. If all the hassle Jayne and I were currently going through meant anything, then I hoped that we would end up having a secure old-age. If that happened then it would be worth it.

***

There was a property agent who some of the guys had used before so I gave him a call. He had a place in mind and took me to see it after work one evening.

It was a small but very well presented one-bedroomed apartment in Joseph Platz. It had a nice living room that had been furnished with some trendy pine furniture. It was all very neat and tidy and I thought that it would be perfect for Jayne, George and me.

I decided to take it and he set about sorting out the paperwork. Just as we were leaving, he said,

"Phone, you will need a phone. I can sort this out for you."

I hadn't really thought about it but he went through his briefcase and produced a form that he filled in and I signed. He then drove me back to Ron's apartment.

***

Time was passing and now that we were going to put our belonging into storage it was important that we threw out as much as possible. There was a council tip a few miles away in Alloa and we made plenty of trips there. It was a little disappointing when we came across some boxes that we hadn't opened the whole time that we had lived in Scotland.

In the garage I found the old gas heater that we had used

when we lived in the old cottage before moving into our house. It belonged to the previous tenant who worked as a shepherd and had kindly left it behind for us to use.

I'd taped his phone number on inside of the door of the heater and decided to give him a call.

"Hi, my name is Harry and I rented the cottage that you used to live in a couple of years ago."

"Yes, I remember."

"Do you remember that you leant us your portable gas heater?"

"Yes."

"Well, we still have it but unfortunately we are now about to move out and we would like to return it to you."

"That's great, thank you for taking the trouble to let me know."

"No problem. I must apologise for not returning it sooner. Would you like a little something for your trouble?"

"No, there is no need for that."

"That's very kind of you. I don't believe that the gas bottle is full so I'll get a new one for you."

"That would be great, thanks."

"You're welcome. Thanks again, it was very useful when we lived there."

I gave him our address and he said that he would pop round to pick it up later in the week which he did. Unfortunately, I wasn't there when he turned up to collect the heater but I felt good that I'd done the right thing by returning it to its rightful owner, complete with full gas bottle.

***

We'd made the decision to put our belongings in storage in Milton Keynes rather than leave it in Scotland. There was no logical reason for this and it would have probably been cheaper to find somewhere in Scotland but it was psychologically comforting knowing that are belongings were 'local' even if we weren't.

I'd already booked a flight from Munich to Edinburgh

and was due to change at Manchester so we organized things so that Jayne would drive 'down south' on the same day and pick me up at Manchester airport.

I was a bit apprehensive as I waited for her to arrive. She was a little late and I had no way of contacting her so there was nothing else for me to do but sit and wait. Eventually she turned up with George. I said,

"Thank God for that, I was beginning to get a bit worried."

"Sorry, there were some roadworks that slowed us down a bit."

"No problem, I'm glad you made it. How did the packing up of the house go?"

"It went really well; they were very efficient. It felt a bit strange staying in an empty house last night but it's all done now."

"Let's hope that the estate agent can sell the house."

"Well, we haven't had any viewers in the last couple of weeks."

"That's a shame."

We made our way to the car and headed towards the M6 motorway. I knew that Jayne would have organised things brilliantly but I was nervous that we now owned an empty house which I felt was a bit of a risk.

***

We spent a hectic weekend visiting family and friends before flying out to Munich on the Monday morning. We went straight to Joseph Platz and I was relieved that Jayne really liked the apartment,

"It's a lot better than some of the other places you've taken me to live in before Harry."

"I thought that you'd like it. It's a bit small but its fine for the three of us."

Jayne had bought a small 'blow up' airbed which was what George was going to sleep on in our room. This worked out really well and he soon settled in.

It was great to be a together again and the apartment

quickly changed from being a bachelor pad to a family home. It certainly needed a woman's touch and we quickly settled into family life again.

***

I was a bit worried that Jayne might be a bit bored being cooped up in the small apartment whilst I was at work all day. Occasionally she would meet me for lunch and we would walk over to 'the lake' restaurant and enjoy some traditional German food. The weather was glorious and it felt a bit like we were on holiday as we sat outside in the sunshine.

Jayne often spent some time exploring Munich. One day whilst pushing George around in his buggy she stumbled upon an 'English shop' which was tucked away down a side-street. Here it was possible to purchase some non-perishable 'British staples" that can easily be taken for granted until you are unable to buy them.

The shop had a notice board that contained lots of interesting information that people thought would be useful to British expats. There were also some personal adds that said things like,

"Mum and baby would like to meet similar for coffee."

"Please phone number attached."

These messages tended to be in the middle of a piece of paper and around the edges the originator had written their phone number multiple times. They'd used some scissors to cut around the number so that it could easily be detached.

This was a simple and yet brilliant idea as it meant that anyone who was interested didn't have to search for a pen. Jayne pulled off a couple numbers that interested her and put them in her purse. She then wrote her own advertisement and put down the phone number of our apartment.

***

I was enjoying family life I was really pleased that Jayne was settling in to living in Germany so well. Unfortunately, the apartment didn't have a traditional oven, but it did have a microwave. This suited me as my culinary skills are extremely limited but for Jayne this was a real challenge. She was a great cook and really loved baking. One day whilst out shopping she spotted a small portable oven for sale so she decided to buy it.

When I saw the oven, I thought it was a silly idea as it was just so small but Jayne had other ideas. I decided not to make a big deal about it but accepted that I wouldn't be getting a 'Sunday roast' anytime soon.

***

It didn't take long before Jayne was contacted by a few mums and slowly but surely, she built up her own social network. This was a really good thing to do as it got her out of the apartment and George was able to interact with other children.

To try and save money the mums would often visit each other's apartments for coffee and a few treats. Due to the different nationalities of the mums they would cook or bake different things, often reflecting their own nationalities.

Rather than host a coffee morning, Jayne decided to invite everyone round for a traditional English 'Cream tea' with scones and cakes. This went down very well and the group encouraged her to do it again which she did.

Jayne also got to know some of the wives of people I worked with which was nice for everyone. I didn't really think about how Jayne was going get on in Germany when she agreed to come over but these things have a tendency to sort themselves out.

***

I got home from work and Jayne said,

"I've got some bad news."

I immediate looked at George but he seemed happy enough so I let Jayne continue.

"Our neighbour in Scotland has sent us a letter and she said that our house has been broken into."

"You're joking!"

"No, they broke a window in the downstairs bedroom at

the back of the house and climbed in. There doesn't appear to be any other damage."

"The bastards."

"Well, they must have been disappointed when they got in because there was nothing to steal."

"So, it was a good idea to put all of our stuff into storage then."

"Absolutely."

"You see, people know if a house is empty. Word travels fast and it would be an easy target."

"She said that they contacted a glazier and the window has been fixed now."

"That was kind of her; we must owe her some money."

"She said that the company will send us an invoice."

"I wonder if the window is still open as she doesn't have a key to the house."

"I don't know but I'll contact the estate agent and ask them to check it next time they are doing a 'viewing'."

"That won't be happening anytime soon then," I replied sarcastically.

"You never know."

Several days letter an invoice from the glazing company duly arrived. I was shocked that it cost around £230 quid with a large portion of that being the 'call-out charge'. I phoned them up to ask why they charged so much but gave up in the end as I didn't know what work had been done. I reluctantly paid it.

***

I found out that my best friend Freddie (who was my best man when I got married) was temporarily working in Basel in Switzerland. Basel was only a three-hour train ride away so we arranged to visit him one weekend. Freddie and I met on our first day at secondary school when we were eleven years old. We hit it off straightaway and have been good friends ever since.

One Friday afternoon, straight after work we made our way to the Hauptbahnhof in Munich. We had bought our train tickets earlier in the week so all we had to do was to find the correct Bahnsteig (platform). Looking at the huge screen we soon found out what platform we had to go to and when we got there, I was delighted to see that our train was going to be an 'ICE' train.

The 'ICE' train (InterCity Express) was a sleek modern beast of a train. It was painted in brilliant white with the red 'DB' (Deutsch Bahn) logo on the side. Walking along the platform I was in awe of this brilliant piece of German engineering. It was like a resting monster waiting to be released.

We placed our luggage in the special compartment near the door and I carried George down the carriage to our allocated seats. I was pleased when I found that we had a table.

The train moved off very gently and it didn't take long for it to build up a good 'head of steam'. We flew along and I felt it was more like being on an aeroplane than a train. George soon got bored with sitting down and Jayne and I did our best to entertain him. However, I ended up walking up and down the carriage holding his hand very tightly.

It was fortuitous that we didn't have to make any changes which made the journey a lot easier. When we got to Basel, Freddie was waiting for us which was a huge relief. He had a big smile on his face as we made our way over to him.

Freddie was working as an aircraft technician at a nearby airport. His company had rented him a two-bedroom apartment for the duration of his assignment which was perfect for us. However, the thing that impressed Jayne the most was not the apartment itself; it was the smell.

Freddie put me to shame as he was a brilliant cook. Knowing that we were coming to stay he had prepared his signature dish which was a superb chicken curry. It smelt fantastic and we didn't waste any time tucking in.

"How come Freddie is such a good cook and you struggle to boil an egg?" Jayne said to me sarcastically.

"I just never got into cooking."

"Your mother obviously spoilt you something rotten."

"It's just something that doesn't interest me."

"Where did you learn to cook like this Freddie?"

"Oh, I just had a go and kept on experimenting."

"Well this is delicious."

"Thanks Jayne, I'm glad you like it."

I felt a little inadequate but that was how things were. Cooking just wasn't my thing and that was that. Freddie took Jayne complements in his stride and I could tell he was pleased that his cooking had been so well received and that was fair enough.

George was put to bed with his bottle and we ended up siting around the table drinking beer having a good old catch-up.

The next day Freddie drove us to Lucerne. This was a beautiful historic place surrounded by impressive mountains. It had a seaside feel about it due to its close proximity to the lake but unfortunately for us the cloud cover was so low that we couldn't see the mountains.

There was an interesting covered wooden bridge that dated back to medieval times. The internal walls were normally pleasantly decorated with some interesting relics but these had recently been removed for some essential maintenance.

We walked around pushing George in his buggy. At the southern side of the bridge we were stalked by some very hungry seagulls. They were interested in any person who was eating anything that they could pilfer. Chips seemed to be a particular 'plunder of choice'.

We watched the gulls for a moment and Freddie said to me,

"I know that they are sometimes classed as vermin but you've got to admire their aviation ability."

"Do you know, I hadn't really thought about it before but yes, they are brilliant flyers."

Freddie drove us back to Basil but before we got to his

apartment, we stopped off at a restaurant to get something to eat. We'd decided to treat Freddie to a meal to thank him for his hospitality. I was just about used to Munich prices but this was unbelievable. I just couldn't see why basic things cost so much money in Switzerland.

When we got back to the apartment Jayne settled George down for the night. She then kindly offered to stay in whilst Freddie and I went out for a beer.

"Are you sure?" I asked.

"Absolutely, it's been a great but long day. You two go out and I'll look after George."

"Okay then, we won't be long."

It was very generous of Jayne to do this, but I could see that she was tired. I just hoped that George didn't play up but I felt that it wouldn't be long before he was fast asleep.

Sitting in a bar Freddie and I spoke openly and honestly about life. We'd been friends for so long that we could talk about anything. He was also good fun and often a little cheeky. However, I got the impression that he was a bit lonely living in Basel on his own but he had just asked a German girl out who worked in the office so he was as optimistic as ever.

*

The next day we decided to leave straight after breakfast. Freddie drove us to the railway station and we said our goodbyes. It had been a really enjoyable weekend and Freddie had been very accommodating. You can't beat the company of old friends and Freddie was the best friend I had.

I was a little bit worried about his lifestyle as I was only too aware of the challenges of living alone in a foreign country.

It was a long time before I saw him again because he moved on to work at another airport not long after that get-together.

The date with the German girl went very well because they ended up getting married and now have two lovely children.

***

CHAPTER 7:

CONTINENTAL TRAVELLERS.

Jayne and I were beginning to feel a little cooped up in the small apartment so we decided to hire a car one weekend. We wanted to go a bit further than Salzburg this time and after much deliberation, we decided to visit the ancient Italian city of Verona.

Verona is over 260 miles to the south of Munich and although the autobahns were extremely good, I knew that our route would take us through Austria and over the Alps.

I took the Friday afternoon off work. We'd hired an Opel Astra from a small garage that wasn't very far from our apartment and went to collect it. The young man who handed the keys over to us was really friendly and enthusiastic about the car.

"We have had all sorts of cars here, Mercedes, BMW's but we have found that Opel give us less problems."

"That's interesting," I replied.

"Well, that is everything sorted for you."

"Thanks for all your help."

"No problem."

I reversed the car and waved to him and then as I pulled forward, he shouted,

"Gute fahrt."

I nearly burst out laughing but just about managed to keep a straight face.

"Do they really say that?" said Jayne as we drove off.

"He just did. I had to look away as I didn't want to laugh."

"Well, he was a very helpful chap."

"Indeed, it was interesting what he said about the different cars they have used over the years. I would have thought that renting out German brands would have been a 'no brainer', especially as we are here in Munich but apparently that is not the case."

"It sounded like they've tried them all out."

"Yes, and I suppose that reliability is key in their business."

"Well, we have had our own Vauxhall Astra a few years now and that's been a really good car."

"You're not wrong. I mean, how many times have I driven up and down the M6 commuting to and from Scotland?"

"I don't know, it must be dozens."

"Yes, and it never let me down."

"I must admit that I was surprised that you hired an Astra."

"Well, it was such a good deal and to be fare it is a newer model than ours."

"It seems a bit smaller than our car but I'm not sure it is."

"Well, it's big enough for what we want. It's interesting that they have called this model an Astra and yet have kept Opel as the manufacturer. Previously Astra's models had been called Kadetts in Germany."

"Perhaps they are consolidating their brand names?"

"It looks like it. Someone at work said to me that Germans like buying German products although Vauxhall and Opel are owned by the American company General Motors."

We made our way out of Munich and headed south towards Austria. We passed some beautiful mountain scenery as we made our way through the Alps. I would have loved to have had time to explore the countryside a bit more. There were some tunnels that we had to go through so I took it steady.

"Do you know anything about Verona?" I said to Jayne.

"I know that it has an ancient amphitheater there that dates back to Roman Times and there is a play by William Shakespeare called 'the two gentlemen of Verona."

"I've heard that they still use the Amphitheatre today. I assume that it's open-air?"

"I would have thought so but that won't be a problem because the weather is not like it is in England."

"I wonder if they perform Shakespeare's play's there?"

"I think it's mostly used for opera but who knows; I bet it would be a good draw if they did. Did you know that there is another Shakespeare play that is set in Verona?"

"Is there? I can see that you went to a better school than I did. Go on then what's it called?"

"Romeo and Juliet."

"That's got to be one of his most famous plays. I knew that it was set in Italy but didn't know exactly where."

"What Shakespeare play did you do at school?"

"Interestingly another famous one set in Italy; Julius Caesar but before you say anything, I'm not driving all the way to Rome."

*

Verona was extremely busy and Jayne and I both scanned all the buildings as we drove along looking for somewhere to stay. In the end we spotted a hotel which was on the main dual-carriageway not far from the centre of Verona. We parked down a side street and I left Jayne and George in the car while I made my way to the hotel.

It was getting late and I was relieved when they said that that had a room available. I promptly paid for two nights and then made my way back to the car to collect Jayne and George.

"Was it expensive?" enquired Jayne.

"No, not really considering it's in the city centre but at

least we now have somewhere to stay."

"Good, I'll sort George out and you can get the bags out of the back of the car."

"Okay."

*

It was clearly a very old hotel and we were both surprised how dilapidated it was. Everything seemed 'a little tired' but this somehow added to its charm. I thought that it would have been very grand in its day.

We quickly settled into our room and I opened the door to the balcony which was a little 'stiff' to say the least. The first thing that struck me was the noise of the traffic; it was terrible. I then realized that we were on one of the city's main access roads. I stepped out nervously as although it looked solid enough it was like the rest of the building and need some serious TLC.

*

We decided to venture out and get something to eat. It was still very warm as we walked up the busy street pushing George in his buggy. It didn't take us long to get to a large open space known as 'Piazza Bra'. We followed the main pedestrian route that had many restaurants to one side which gave its diners a magnificent view of the Piazza with its established trees, monuments and fountains.

"It's nice to get away from the traffic for a bit isn't it?" said Jayne.

"Yes, but I'm surprised how many people there are walking about."

"Well, this is obviously the place to be."

There were lots of restaurants at the edge of the perimeter of the Piazza which was where most people were heading. It was tempting to do a bit more exploring but we decided to get something to eat first.

It was extremely busy but eventually we managed to get an outside table which offered a great view of the amphitheatre. We ordered a couple of beers along with some traditional Italian lasagna for both Jayne and I. While we waited for it to arrive, we turned George to face us in his buggy and Jayne fed him some food that she had prepared earlier.

"What a view."

"Yes, it is; I can't quite believe that we are actually here."

"I know what you mean; it's a bit different from Milton Keynes."

"Just a bit. The history here is amazing."

"I can't believe how many people there are walking about."

"Yes, and they are all so well dressed."

"There must be something going on although I cannot see anything in the amphitheatre."

Our food arrived and Jayne gave George a toy to play with whilst we tucked in. When we finished our meal, we ordered a couple more beers and just relaxed and took in the atmosphere.

We still couldn't get over how many people were walking about. It was tempting to follow them but we had such a good seat which we didn't want to lose.

Jayne and I were both really tired and just appreciated sitting down. It was then that Jayne said something,

"Do you see that man in the blue top? He just walked past us a few moments ago going in the other direction."

"Did he?"

"Yes, and that group of girls."

I looked over but didn't recall them. I was just about to dismiss what she had said but then I recognised two people that I had seen earlier.

"I do recognise that couple there."

"So, what are we seeing here?"

"Well, I would guess that they aren't actually going anywhere. They are walking up and down."

"That's a bit strange don't you think."

"Well, they all look immaculately dressed, I guess that they are just 'strutting their stuff', Italians like style and fashion."

Spotting people we'd already seen became a bit of a sport for us but we soon got tired of it and settled the bill before heading back to our hotel.

*

The next day we had a great breakfast. George was being a little cheeky and kept on walking around the restaurant. He went up to an elderly gentleman and grabbed his hand. Fortunately, he was a very kind man and let George take him for a walk. He then turned to us and said in a very deep American accent,

"I hope you don't mind but your son wants to show me around."

"As long as that's okay with you?"

"Not at all, he's a very determined little chap."

"You're not wrong there."

George was 'full of himself' and both Jayne and I didn't have a clue where he got his confidence from. Fortunately, he soon got bored and came back to us. I told him to say thank you to the kind gentleman which he did.

"You're very welcome young man," replied the gentleman.

We put George in his buggy, gave him a toy to play with and continued our conversation.

"Are you sure you're up for this trip?"

"I know that we have only just got here but it's somewhere I have always wanted to visit and we can still do some more exploring here tomorrow."

"I think it will be a two-hour drive."

"But we have the hire car so we may as well use it."

"Okay, we'd better make tracks then."

We managed to navigate our way without too much hassle but as we got nearer, I became a little concerned that perhaps it would have been a better idea to go by train. I knew that Venice didn't have any cars so I was really concerned about where we would park when we got there.

I'd spent a day in Venice before as I'd stopped off there when I travelled around Europe by train (Inter-Rail). This was ten years or so previously and long before I met Jayne. I planned that trip so that I could save money by sleeping on trains wherever I could. I never for one moment thought that one day I would be driving there with my wife and young son in the car.

Venice is an island and to get there we had to drive over a long bridge that ran parallel with the railway. Fortunately, Jayne spotted a parking sign and as we got closer, I could see a multi-story carpark.

We drove up the levels of the carpark but couldn't find any empty spaces. I was beginning to get a bit worried, if we couldn't find somewhere to park, we had no choice but to drive out of the city and back over that long bridge. I didn't have a plan 'B'.

Driving up a ramp we suddenly found ourselves in glorious sunshine. Obviously, this meant that we were at the top floor. I drove around the circuit and had just about given up hope when a car nudged forward. I couldn't believe my luck so I waited politely for him to leave and promptly drove straight into his vacant space.

Normally I would have reversed in but I was not in the mood to take a chance. I didn't want the car behind nicking my spot. If he was angry that I'd got the only available place he didn't indicate this but I wondered if he cursed us Germans as we had a German number plate.

I watched him drive past us in the rearview mirror before opening my door. I had a really good stretch before getting the buggy out of the back. Jayne got George out of the car and put him in the buggy and we made our way towards the lift.

"I couldn't believe it when we got that space," I said to Jayne.

"You're not wrong. We could have been there ages."

"Well we're here now so let's make the most of it."

It was a glorious day and Venice was extremely atmospheric. It was hard going with a buggy as there were several small footbridges over the canals that we had to negotiate but it was peaceful because there weren't any cars.

Looking around it appeared to me that Venice was falling to bits, all the buildings looked dilapidated but somehow this just added to its charm. It really is a truly unique place.

We didn't have a map but there were plenty of signs pointing to St. Mark's square. Every so often I turned to look back the way we had come and tried to make a mental note of any landmarks which would help me remember the route as obviously we would have to find the carpark again.

Eventually we found ourselves in St. Mark's Square and it was truly magnificent. It was extremely busy and there were people everywhere. We made our way to the water's edge and then on to the famous 'bridge of sighs'.

Back in the square we visited the famous church.

It was time for a sit down and a coffee and there was a restaurant in the square that had lots of seats outside so we sat down and looked at the menu. The prices were extortionate but it must have been one of the best locations for a restaurant in the world.

Normally I wouldn't have given the restaurant a second thought but we really needed a sit down so we found a table with a nice umbrella and made ourselves comfortable. The waitress came over and I ordered a couple of coffees. They were without doubt the most expensive coffees that I'd ever ordered but here we were so I just took being ripped-off 'on the chin'.

George didn't appreciate the posh restaurant, the architecture or the surroundings. He was understandably fed up with being in his buggy. We tried to entertain him as best we could whilst we drank our coffees but there was only one thing that interested him and that was the pigeons.

I unbuckled him and held his hand as we walked over to the huge flock of pigeons that were swarming around trying to obtain any 'titbits' that they could find. He pulled on my arm but as we got nearer the birds just scurried away in different directions.

George wasn't impressed with this and walked faster and faster tugging at my hand with all his might but the birds were far too quick for him. In the end I decided to let go of his hand and he ran towards some birds as quickly as he could.

Some the birds noted his increase in speed and decided to 'take off'; this motivated the others to do the same even though they were well out of George's range. The result of this 'bird-panic' was swathes of birds flying around.

People ducked as the birds swooped over them and what only a moment ago had been a beautiful tranquil picturesque scene in one of the prettiest places in the world now became total mayhem which had all been started by a little boy trying to play with some pigeons.

I grabbed hold of him and 'frog-marched' him back to Jayne. I told him off but all he had been trying to do was play with the birds, he didn't realise that he had done anything wrong.

The birds eventually came back and life returned to normal. I decided to go to the toilet and went into the restaurant. I made my way to the Gents and was annoyed when the lady expected a tip. I put some coins into a china saucer and left as quickly as I could before she came running after me complaining that it wasn't enough.

We settled George down back at our table by giving him something to eat and ordered two more coffees. Expensive as it was, we knew that it would be a long time before we would be visiting Venice again.

It was a nice moment, sitting in St. Mark's square. There was a real sense of 'presence' about the place and just when we thought that it couldn't get any better a quartet started playing some beautiful classical musical. Jayne informed me it was Mozart and the whole experience became even more magical.

*

We paid the bill and I held George's hand as we walked around the square. At the far end there were less people about so I decided to let him go so that he could chase some more pigeons. He thought that this was great fun and it didn't cause as much of a problem as it had done previously.

"Do you think he'll get tired of that?" said Jayne.

"I doubt it. I just hope he doesn't catch one."

"I don't know, here we are in a very special place and all he is interested in is the pigeons."

"I'm hoping that it wears him out a bit before we have to put him back in the car."

"I don't think anything will every wear him out."

We continued to walk around the perimeter of the square and then successfully navigated our way back to the car.

***

Back in Verona I went down to the hotel bar and ordered two red wines which I put on a small tray. I found it slightly difficult navigating my way back to our room carrying them but paying for room service just isn't in my DNA.

When I got back to the room, I could see that George was safely tucked up in bed with a nice warm bottle of milk. I walked out onto the balcony and put the drinks down on the table.

"It's a bit noisy out here isn't it?"

"It sure is."

"Trust us to get a room facing the road."

"I didn't think to ask what rooms were available; I just went for the cheapest one that they had."

"No change there then."

"Well, you know how it is."

"It reminds me of the hotel we stayed at in Athens. That was on a busy street too."

"Indeed, it was. I'd forgotten about that; what a few days that was."

"Whose idea was it to make that crazy trip?"

"You know it was my idea, I thought that we could see a bit more of Greece whilst we were there."

"But we were in Corfu. How many people go on holiday to Corfu and end up getting an overnight bus to Athens?"

"Not many but we made it."

"Only just."

"I must admit it was a bit of an adventure."

"That's an understatement if ever I heard one. I thought it would be a straightforward journey but that coach driver drove like a maniac."

"He does it every day so he knew what he was doing."

"But we didn't. When he raced down to the docks, I thought he was on a suicide mission and that we were going to end up in the water."

"I must admit I was a bit worried then."

"A bit worried! I was bloody terrified and when he drove straight up the ramp and on to that boat, I was convinced that we were going to crash."

Jayne picked up her wine glass and took a sip before continuing,

"I mean, no one told us that we were late for a ferry, if you could call it that. I had absolutely no idea what was going on."

The ferry that Jayne was referring to looked like an old World War II landing craft that was moored at the dock with its ramp down. It was full of vehicles and foot passengers but they had left enough room for the bus which they were patiently waiting for so that it could set sail.

"It was worse than fairground ride."

"But it was nice sailing across the water in the middle of the night once we'd recovered from the trauma."

"Did we ever recover? I think I'm suffering from post-traumatic stress disorder just thinking about it."

The adventure didn't end when we got to Athens's bus station in the early hours of the morning. We asked a taxi-driver if he knew of a hotel which he did so we let him take us there. I concentrated really hard trying to memorise the route.

"And when we got to the hotel we couldn't sleep

because the traffic was so noisy and it was just so hot."

"I remember, we got up and made our way to the Acropolis."

"Which was shut after we walked all the way there and climbed up that hill?"

"Yes, but we weren't to know that where we?"

"And later in the evening we made our way back to the bus station so that we could reserve our seats for the journey back and what happened when we got there? They said that there were no buses after today until further notice because they were on strike. So, we had no choice but to go back to the hotel and travel back to Corfu that night but there was a problem wasn't there. We couldn't remember the name of the hotel we were staying in, could we?"

Jayne paused and looked at me sternly.

"But we did use our initiative."

"You were so lucky that you found a cab driver who was prepared to take us to an unspecified destination."

"I probably made his day. It must have been the nearest thing to 'follow that car' that he had ever heard from a customer."

"I bet he only accepted us because he thought he would make a killing."

"Yes, but I don't know how I did it but I managed to remember the route. I knew that if we didn't follow it exactly, we would have been in real trouble. There was no plan 'B', we had to follow the exact same route that we had just walked."

"It was funny watching you telling him which way to go, especially with all those hand gestures."

"He was a real good sport and is probably still telling the story of two crazy English backpackers who navigated him through Athens."

"It was good that we were able to check-out of the hotel so quickly too."

"Yes, but we had to pay for the night that we didn't use."

"We had no choice, if we didn't get back to Corfu that

night, we would have missed our flight back home."

"Do you remember the taxi driver who took us back to the bus station from the hotel?"

"How could I forget him?"

"He didn't want to take us to the bus station, did he?"

"No, he wanted to take us to our final destination and kept asking us where that was."

"He was a real 'chancer' wasn't he? I don't think he believed us when we explained that we were traveling all the way to Corfu."

"No, he didn't believe us but, in the end, I think that even he thought that it was possibly a bit too far to go in a taxi."

"Especially as we already had a bus ticket."

"That certainly was a stressful couple of hours."

"I shudder to think what would have happened if we hadn't managed to get on that bus."

"We would still be there now."

"Well, there were no cheap options."

"At least we would have been able to fly back to the UK from Athens as we had all our belongings with us including the tent."

"There weren't any budget airlines around then so it would have been expensive."

"But sometimes you have no choice."

"You're right there."

"Looking back now, it was a bit of an adventure wasn't it?"

"Yes, it was but one that I don't want to experience again."

**

The next morning after an excellent breakfast we again walked up to the amphitheatre and absorbed the atmosphere. It felt even more special because being a Sunday there were lots of bells chiming and people were wearing their 'Sunday best' to go to church. There was lovely relaxing feel about the place.

*

Driving back though Austria reminded me of the many weekends that I'd driven up and down the M6 when I used to commute to Scotland. Things hadn't turned out how we had hoped but our 'new life' certainly had its advantages and it had been nice to make the most of them like being able to spend a lovely weekend in Italy.

***

Back in our apartment I was flicking around the cable TV channels when I stumbled upon a news article that featured St. Mark's square in Venice. I couldn't understand what was being said but it featured an elderly lady mopping the steps of a restaurant. When the camera scanned around, I could see that the whole of St. Mark's square had been flooded. It was a real shame that such a beautiful place was in such danger from the Sea.

***

CHAPTER 8:

OKTOBERFEST.

In the office there was a lot of talk about the world-famous Oktoberfest that was due to be held in Munich. The IT department was going to book a small area one evening. I was a little confused that it was being held in September but someone explained that it runs for nearly three-weeks and finishes on the first weekend in October.

One Sunday lunchtime I had some time to kill whilst waiting for the Sunday Papers at the main railway station so I went and studied a map. It didn't take me long to locate Theresienwiese which was a 'kidney shaped' piece of open ground. I knew that this was the location of Oktoberfest and being only a fifteen-minute walk away so I decided to take a look.

When I got there, I was a little shocked as all I could see was one huge building site. There were lots of cranes that appeared to be assembling a large 'roller coaster'. There were a few people working but not many which surprised me but then I remembered how much the Germans respected Sundays.

My impression was that there was no way that they were going to finish its completion for the start of the festival but they had done this many times before and knew what they were doing.

I decided to walk around the whole site. The image I had of a beer tent that had been put up on a village green had been blown away. The beer tents were more like mini-stadiums and I realised that this was beer distribution on an industrial scale. It certainly wasn't 'small beer'.

I left them to it and made my way back to the railway station. It had been an interesting walk and I was pleased that I'd 'got my bearings' as to where the festival was being held.

*

The following Saturday morning Jayne and I took George to see the beer festival's opening parade. We didn't know what to expect as we joined the crowds who lined the route. Due to the number of people there we soon realised that we weren't going to be able to see very much.

Unfortunately, George didn't like being kept waiting; he kept wriggling in his buggy and wanted to be let out. I felt sure that he would have preferred to have been taken to a park where he could have played on the equipment. In the end we decided to let him out of his buggy. Jayne held his hand tightly as we took him for a walk.

George didn't want to be held and just kept pulling at Jayne's arm but there was no way that she was going to let go of him. We came across a large paved area so I went ahead and turned to face them.

Jayne looked at me and then let him go. His face immediately became one big grin and within a second, he was off. He ran straight towards me and I grabbed him under his arms and swung him around. I placed him gently on the ground and turned him to face Jayne. He then started to run towards Jayne who also grabbed him under the arms and swung him around.

George ran up and down lots of times. He was clearly enjoying himself; this was all he wanted to do. He wasn't bothered that the parade was now in 'full swing' with brass bands marching along at the end of the street.

Eventually he gave up running so Jayne put him back in his buggy and gave him a juice in his red plastic cup that had a moulded 'mouthpiece' so that if he dropped it none of the juice would spill out. We walked back towards the parade but due to the number of people watching all we could see was the tops of the floats as they went by.

I wanted to see the parade and looking around I saw that a shop across the road had some blue tiles below its shop window. There were some horizontal tiles at the base of its window that formed a ledge. I thought that this was large enough for me to stand on so I climbed up and found that I was able to get a good view of the parade as I could see over the crowd.

The whole spectacle was stunning. There were lots of bands, people walking by wearing traditional Bavarian dress and some beautifully decorated horse drawn beer wagons. There was no doubt that we were in Germany and I could see why some people referred to Munich as the 'beer capital of the world'.

We decided that it was time to go into the festival. I wasn't sure if it was going to be a good place to take a child but it was a sunny Saturday afternoon and the atmosphere was more like a fun fair (which it was) than a beer festival.

It was really very busy, there were people everywhere. We passed a group of lads who were dressed in traditional lederhosen which is something that I couldn't see myself ever wearing.

Unbelievably, I spotted a group of people from work who were sitting at a table having a beer in the open air. They were sat outside one of the main beer marquees. There were two empty seats so we grabbed them before anyone else could take them.

It was a good place to sit as you could clearly hear the 'Oompah' band performing in marquee and also watch the world go by.

One of the traditionally dressed waitresses came over and asked what we wanted to drink. I was a little wary of having a beer as I knew that it was strong but in the end Jayne and I decided that we would join in the party so we ordered a 'Mass' each (a litre of beer served in a clear glass).

The waitress duly returned carrying an unbelievable number of heavy glasses. How she managed to carry so many beers was beyond me but she quickly put them down on the table and distributed them to thirsty drinkers.

Once everyone had their drinks, we all stood up and 'prosted' each other. Not to be outdone George picked up his little red two-handled 'baby cup' and promptly joined in. Everyone in turn politely touched their glasses with his little cup. He thought that this was great fun and kept doing it over and over again which got a little tedious to say the least.

We were joined by another colleague and his wife which was nice. They had a young baby with them who was asleep in his pram. They ordered some drinks and were relaxing when their baby woke up.

The baby started to cry very loudly and he turned to me and said,

"Harry, do you know of anywhere around here where you can get baby food?"

I looked at him disbelievingly. His child was obviously hungry and I couldn't believe that he or his wife hadn't bought any baby food with them.

"I haven't a clue mate."

I asked Jayne if she had anything in our bag that would help but she didn't. The baby was getting more fractious so we decided to ask one of the waitresses if they knew of anywhere.

"Why don't you go and ask the kitchen staff, they may be able to help."

"Okay thanks."

We both went to the kitchen but I didn't think that they would have anything that a baby could eat. I couldn't believe how unprepared he was but kept quiet as he asked for some help. Whilst they were talking, he had an idea.

"Is it possible for you to give me some mashed potato with gravy?"

They said that they would be able to do this and it worked a treat. I couldn't believe that he'd managed to sort something out in such a busy place.

I really liked the traditional German dresses that all the waitresses were wearing. They all looked beautifully feminine and it added to the pleasant ambiance of the festival. The design certainly enhanced their 'assets' and the term 'buxom wench' came to mind.

*

We were really enjoying ourselves; everyone was in good spirits. We ended up having another beer and then decided to make our way home.

The weather was sunny and as we walked along. We came across some people who were laying down on an earth-bank. I was a little concerned that they weren't moving and then I realised that they had probably had 'one drink too many' and were sleeping it off.

We made our way home pushing George in his buggy though the crowds. There were people everywhere and I now realised how popular Oktoberfest was. It was a very successful tourist attraction.

*

The next day I plugged my camcorder into the TV. I was pleased with the footage of the parade that I'd taken whilst I stood on the ledge of the shop window whilst Jayne had entertained George.

It all looked really good but then we started to watch a scene where George was sat in in pram enjoying a beef burger. I said to Jayne,

"I don't remember going to McDonald's yesterday."

"Neither do I," replied Jayne.

"Well we did and here's the proof."

We both stared at the TV in disbelief. I'd obviously filmed it and when I zoomed out Jayne was having a little trouble standing and was using George's pram as a support.

"Oh my God. Look at the state of me."

We couldn't believe what we were seeing. Talk about irresponsible parents. We'd both obviously had too much to drink which normally would have been okay but to be responsible for a child at the same time was a little scary to say the least. We felt a little ashamed of ourselves and we both decided that it would never happen again and it never did.

***

The main computer system that our company used was called ManMan (Manufacturing Management). This was the product of an American company called ASK whose software was used throughout the world with about 120 sites located in the UK. I'd used it for several years but I'd mostly written reports using a software tool called 'Quiz'. This software was one component of a 4th Generation computer language called Powerhouse which was supplied by a Canadian company called Cognos.

I naturally assumed that we would be using Powerhouse to develop our software but for some reason they decided to change direction and opted for a similar product call 'Speedware'. I wasn't happy with this choice as I wanted to improve my powerhouse skill rather than have to learn a new computer language.

Once the decision was made to opt for Speedware they arranged for us all to attend a training course. This was a one-week course and would take place in our Munich offices.

A Speedware instructor came out from the UK to run the course. It was an enjoyable week but it wasn't' what I wanted to do. I didn't see the point of learning a language that I thought I would probably never use again.

My experience told me that these languages have their limitations. There was no doubt that they could save you a lot of time but if you wanted to some something really complicated then it was better to write it in COBOL or in our case FORTRAN which was the computer language that the ManMan system was written in.

*

One of our project team was familiar with Speedware, his name was Zaki and he was from Malaysia. He had an endearing persona and was very popular. It was good to have someone who had some real experience of the product.

To bolster the team further, they decided to recruit someone else with Speedware experience and one day a young Scottish chap turned up called Craig. Craig didn't have any ManMan experience but he certainly knew Speedware.

Ken, Zaki and I would be the main software developers working on the project. The project leader was a chap call Elliot. He'd worked on the previous project (ARE - Automatic Repair Exchange) which was the software that I had supported when I worked in Scotland. Elliot had been a contractor for years and had wealth of knowledge and experience.

Munich was the European headquarters of the company but the project was all about the distribution of Spare parts around EMEA (Europe, Middle-East and Africa). The company's new distribution centre was located in Holland which was where the systems main business users also resided.

***

Jayne made a suggestion one evening,

"Why don't you invite a couple of your work colleagues round for dinner one evening?"

"That's a nice idea, what made you think of that?"

"I just thought that it would be nice for me to get to know the people you work with a bit better; I hear a lot about them from what you tell me."

"Okay, I'll invite Craig round. I think he would appreciate a bit of home cooking. Talking of home cooking, how are you going to manage using that little table top oven?"

"That oven is more flexible than you think. Don't you worry about the food, leave that to me. Just let me know who is coming and gave me a little notice."

"Fair enough."

Craig accepted our dinner invitation. Since he started, we had become good friends and as he was an experienced Speedware developer he had taught me a lot which I really appreciated.

There was another programmer there who wasn't working on our project. He was extremely quiet and highly regarded. He had also helped me when I first arrived so I decided to invite him as well.

I didn't know if he was going to accept as socially, he kept himself to himself. I'd been for many a beer after work but he never seemed to join us. When I invited him, he was delighted and accepted immediately which I was really pleased about.

We ended up having several meals together. Jayne as usual excelled in the kitchen and it was really nice sitting around a table having a good old chat. It's hard working away from home and living on your own in a different country so when an offer of a bit of English home cooking comes along then I think it was really appreciated.

**

The team were invited to a project 'kick-off' meeting in Holland so we all left work at midday and made our way to Munich airport.

We were on official business so that meant that the company were paying for our flights. I enjoyed the luxury of travelling business class. It would have been nice to indulge in the champagne that was on offer but I thought better of it. We picked up a hire-car and set off on the hour-long journey to the DCE (Distribution Centre Europe).

Driving though Holland in November 1993, Elliot managed to tune the radio into the England v San Marino football match that was being played at the time. This was a world cup qualifier and we all listened as best we could but unfortunately, the radio reception wasn't very good and neither was England's performance because within a few minutes England were 1 nil down.

*

I remembered the new distribution centre being announced when I worked for the company in Scotland. It was very big news and there was a lot of excitement at the time as it represented the forward-looking approach of the company. I never thought that one day I would actually visit it.

It was interesting meeting everyone. I didn't realise that so many people were involved in the project. One of the team members was a Norwegian chap called Lars. He'd worked in Munich before and was very highly regarded; he also seemed to know everyone.

The project leader certainly knew how to present himself and I thought that it was a very professional meeting. However, I was a little wary of how things were going to turn out. I was new to the Speedware language and still had a lot to learn and it looked like we were all going to be under a lot of pressure to meet the project deadlines.

The project leader had arranged for everyone to have a meal in a nice restaurant straight after work. This was in the town centre and when we found it, we were ushered to the beer garden at the back where a large row of tables had been arranged especially for us.

It was a nicely sheltered area and ideal for a little 'get to know you' event. The weather was warm and the beer was nice and cold.

The meal was really good and we were all getting along very well in a pleasant relaxed environment. Lars went to the toilet and immediately someone produced a couple of black bin liners, he then discretely took some items out of the bin liners and passed them under the table to the people sitting on either side of him.

I didn't have a clue what was going on and a few moments later I was passed something that was made of soft plastic. It appeared to be toy and I soon realised that it was an axe. I didn't know what I was supposed to do with it but I quickly passed it on to the person next to me. I was then passed something that was made of solid plastic. I realised that it was a hat but I daren't look at it as it was obvious that this was all being done covertly.

Lars returned to his seat and as he took a sip of his beer a waitress produced a large cake complete with candles. We all immediately started singing happy birthday. Once he recovered from the shock, he blew the candles out and everyone immediately put on their Viking hats or raised their plastic axes and cheered loudly.

Lars's face was a picture, he hadn't seen this coming at all (and neither had I). It had been an excellently well-timed birthday 'stitch-up'. Once things had calmed down a bit, I found that I could get a bit of a laugh when I twisted my cow horns and pretended that it was a radio antenna.

It was a very good night but I felt that our new Dutch colleagues were a little bit reserved or perhaps they were on their best behaviour. On the other hand, they could have just been more professional than I was.

***

Back in Munich I had a conversation with a colleague on the bus one day. He had a child who was about to start school. The German education system by all accounts is excellent but he was concerned that at some point in time he would have to return home and place his son in a UK school. He was worried about what effect this would have on him.

"The thing his Harry, children grow roots," he said.

"I see what you mean."

"What are you planning to do for your son?"

"We have some time yet; George is only one and a half years old."

"Well, it's something that you need to think about."

I thought about his situation a lot. Finding a school for George hadn't even crossed my mind. We were just grateful that I'd been able to find some work but I knew that sooner or later we would have to make a decision.

***

We received an offer for our house in Scotland which was less than we'd paid for it only two years earlier. It was the first bit of interest that we'd had so in the end we decided to 'take the hit' and accept their offer.

It was frustrating that we'd spent a lot of time and money doing the house up and now all of that was money was 'down the drain' as it hadn't resulted in improving its value.

*

We decided to stay in Munich for Christmas as we didn't see the point of travelling back to the UK when Jayne was planning to return there in January anyway. The house sale had lifted our spirits and Jayne would now be able to do some serious house hunting, especially as we were now 'cash buyers' although I didn't know where we stood regarding getting a mortgage as I was now self-employed.

*

One of the managers that I'd worked with in Scotland had relocated to Munich as a permanent employee. He worked in a different office to me but we'd met up a few times and Jayne and his wife had shared the odd 'coffee morning' together. He was married and had a young daughter who was a few years older than George.

His role in the company was completely different from mine as he was a business manager and a permanent employee but he was very 'down to earth' and I liked him a lot. They rented a house to the east of Daglfing S-Bahn station and they kindly invited us to spend Christmas day with them. This was a really lovely thing to do and we eagerly accepted.

*

Christmastime in Munich was lovely. The whole place had a lovely warm cosy feel about it. I found it difficult to understand why I felt like this and wondered if it was the architecture, the decorations or the wintery conditions. I couldn't 'put my finger on it' but it certainly had a 'togetherness' feel about it and although there was a nice Christmas market in the centre it still felt a lot less commercialised than it does in the UK.

It didn't surprise me that the S-Bahn worked a normal service on Christmas Day so Jayne and I had no trouble getting to our friend's house. It was a very pleasant day and they had gone to a lot of trouble. The dinner was superb and once everything was cleared away, we played some games with the children.

They suggest that we went out for a walk. Not very far from where they lived was a horse race track and there were a few races being held on Christmas day.

I know nothing about horse racing but was happy to go along with everyone. When we got there, I realised that it wasn't a traditional horse racing event as the riders wouldn't be sitting on the horse, they would be sitting on a trap behind it. This meant that they wouldn't be galloping but trotting.

The track was called Daglfing Trabrennbahn, which means 'trotting course'. To be honest I found the thought of a 'trotting race' a little uninspiring but as I watched I could see that it was more about skill than speed. Overdo it and the trap could easily turn over.

We only stayed for a few races which was long enough to experience something new. I really enjoyed it and it was good to get some fresh air although it was rather cold.

When we returned to their house Jayne took control of the kitchen and promptly used up some of the Christmas dinner 'leftovers' by recooking it all in a large frying pan. This was then served 'piping hot' with some pickle and ketchup.

It was nice to eat something hot after our walk in the cold air. It was also nice that Jayne did a bit of cooking and introduced our Scottish friends to the English tradition that is 'Bubble and Squeak'.

***

Jayne was a little disappointed that I went into the office for the three working days between Christmas and New Year. There was no real need for me to do this but it was an opportunity for me to get some work done when there wasn't much going on.

I enjoyed being in the office as there weren't many people about and it gave me an opportunity to learn a bit more about the system and to experiment with the Speedware computer language.

Jayne met up with some of her friends in the morning and then made her way to the office with George and we went out for lunch. This made things a bit easier for both of us as it broke the day up nicely.

***

Jayne and I decided to stay in our apartment to see in the New Year as there was little chance of getting a baby sitter. I bought a bottle of German Sekt which we both liked and I already had a malt whisky that I'd purchased from Duty Free on one of my many trips back to the UK.

Our quiet New Year's evening didn't last long as the street below us became very noisy with revellers shouting and setting off fireworks. We looked out of our window and watched everyone enjoying themselves. It was a shame that we didn't have a balcony. George somehow managed to sleep through all the 'din' which was amazing.

When the New Year arrived, I became a bit emotional, a year earlier we were living in Scotland awaiting a redundancy cheque and now I had a well-paid contract in the heart of Europe. We'd survived a tumultuous year and things had turned out far better than we could possibly have dreamed of.

Our future was still very uncertain but one thing we did know was that 'god willing' there was going to be a new member of our family arriving in 1994.

Gute Fahrt

***

CHAPTER 9:

A NEW COUNTRY.

I was walking down the corridor on my way to the small kitchen when I overheard a conversation,

"Have you seen our share price today?"

"No."

"It's the highest it's been for three years."

"Really, I wonder what's caused that."

"Well, I know that we've been making good progress lately but it's gone through the roof."

I made my brew and returned to my desk. Looking at the screen on my PC I could see that the share price had indeed gone up. I'd never seen it at that level and as I was thinking about it a thought popped into my head.

When I joined the company as a permanent employee exactly three years ago, I was allocated a generous amount of share-options. The price of these shares (the strike price) was the price on the day that I joined which at the time was very high. Unfortunately, it didn't take long before they crashed and they never reached my strike price the whole time I worked for them as a permanent employee.

The way the process worked was that you could sell your shares at any time and would profit from the difference between your strike price and your selling price. Your profit was subject to US tax. I was amazed that it was now above my strike price for the first time which was a good thing as it reflected the health of the company.

Over the years many employees had made a lot of money on this scheme as the company had grown and become more successful. I'd given up hope of making a profit and had completely forgotten about them. It was annoying but there was nothing I could do about it now and had to accept that this 'nice little earner' had passed me by.

Several days later I was having a conversation with a small group and the share price was mentioned. Everyone seemed very happy about it and were talking about how they were going to spend their 'windfall'.

I was a little depressed and then I said,

"It's now above my strike price so if I was still a permanent employee then I would be making some money which never happened the whole time I worked in Scotland."

"Harry, when did you leave the company?"

"About ten months ago."

"Well I seem to remember that your options are valid for one year after you leave the company."

"Are you sure?"

"I'm sure I read it somewhere."

"How can I find out?"

"Go and see HR, they would be able to confirm it. I assume that it's the same for us here in Munich as it was for you guys in Scotland."

"Thanks, I'll go and check."

*

My HR contacts in Scotland were no longer with the company so I ventured 'upstairs' to where the HR department was.

"Hello, can I help you?"

"Yes, my name is Harry and I work downstairs in IT."

"I'm pleased to meet you Harry."

"I used to be a permanent employee with the company

and I was wondering if you could clarify something for me?"

"I'll try."

I told her what I had found out and she quickly replied,

"My understanding is that the rules are the same for everyone."

She then went to a filing cabinet and gave me a form.

"I would recommend that you fill this in and fax it to the number on the top. You can specify here how many shares you want to sell."

I looked down at where she was pointing.

"I want to sell all of them but I don't have much time before they expire so I hope that there isn't a backlog in the processing of these forms."

"I would recommend that you add a covering letter saying that it's urgent then."

"That's a good idea. Thank you so much, you have been a great help."

"You're very welcome."

I took the form back to my desk and read it thoroughly. There wasn't much to it and I was lucky that for some strange reason I remembered exactly how many options I'd been given so it was very easy to fill in.

I then needed to find a fax machine and shouted out,

"Does anyone know where there is a fax machine?"

Someone replied, "There's one on the top floor where the executives reside."

"Thanks, I'll try and find it."

I went to the top floor and realised that this was a different world. It was just so quiet; there wasn't the 'hustle and bustle" of the 'shop floor' where I worked. I did a quick scan as I walked around and then I spotted a fax machine in an office which appeared to be occupied by a secretary to one of the company executives.

I knocked on the door and asked,

"Excuse me, I need to send this fax urgently and wondered if it would be possible to use your machine?"

"Is it for company business?"

"Well, kind of."

"Excuse me."

"Well, I need to send this to our headquarters in America and I've only a short time before my share options expire."

"That's fine then, please help yourself and remember that you need to dial '9' to get an outside line."

I went over to the machine, placed the form in the feeder, dialed the number and waited. I could see the executive's office through the open door. He was sat at a huge desk and everything seemed immaculate. There was even a posh cup and saucer. I tried to not make it obvious that I was having a good look as his secretary was keeping an eye on me to make sure I was behaving myself.

Once the machine had done its work, I waited for the acknowledgement slip to be printed. I couldn't see any problems so I assumed that everything was okay. I then picked up my form and said,

"Thank you so much. You've been a great help."

"You're welcome."

I turned and left the office. I was grateful that I'd been allowed to use the fax machine but I really felt uncomfortable standing there. I didn't belong in their world of image and power.

*

Sitting at my desk I couldn't believe that I'd been so lucky to find out that I could still sell my shares. If I hadn't overheard that conversation I would have been 'none the wiser'.

I knew that timing was now everything and I hoped that they would process my form ASAP but it was all out of my control. I thought about phoning them up to check that that had received my form but didn't really want to make a call to America.

I reflected on the other two hundred and fifty members of staff who had been made redundant a year earlier. I wondered how many of them didn't know that they had a year after leaving to sell their shares.

Unfortunately, there was no way of getting in contact with my ex-colleagues. I thought about contacting the Scottish HR department but even if they could help, I wasn't sure that there was enough time. It was a shame that no-one had mentioned this during the long five months redundancy notice period. I'd attended many useful sessions and didn't recall it ever being mentioned. Unfortunately, it was now too late to do anything about it.

I'd taken the decision to work an extra week in Scotland, this was to help with the warehouse move but it also allowed me to attend the last day of a business course that I was doing in Alloa. This now turned out to be a great decision as if I hadn't have done that then I would definitely not have been able to sell my shares in time. What a pleasant twist of fate that had turned out to be.

***

I wasn't involved in the decision-making aspect of the project but it became clear to me that there was a bit of a 'power play' going on. The project leader was based in Holland at the DCE (Distribution Centre Europe) and he had decided to use a Dutch software house to assist him with the project.

My feeling was that if they could, the software house would have bought in their own computer programmers to write the software but this wasn't possible as we were already doing this work here in Munich. It soon transpired that they wanted us to relocate to Holland.

The thought of moving to Holland didn't bother me too much. I knew that it would be a bit of an upheaval but I was still grateful for the work and decided to just go along with things.

***

We had a nice dinner in the apartment and I said to Jayne,

"It looks like they want to move the team to Holland."

"When's that going to happen then?"

"Once it's been confirmed I would say very quickly. You know what it's like once these decisions have been made. I think that they want more control over the software development."

"Can you refuse to go?"

"Not really, I'm a contractor now so I have to go where they send me."

"What about us?"

"We need to decide what we want to do. I'm just letting you know what they are saying at work, we will just have to see what happens."

*

It did indeed turn out that they wanted us to relocate to Holland and they wanted the move completed as quickly as possible. There were a lot of things to sort out and when I told Jayne she said,

"Well you did say that this might be happening."

"I know but they could have given us a bit more notice."

"Where will you stay?"

"I don't know. There is a motel near the distribution centre and I know that a few of the guys have stayed there when they needed to. It's not very luxurious but I guess it's cheap and cheerful."

"I'll tell you what, George and I will go back to the UK straightaway. There's no point in us being here if you are off to Holland."

"Are you sure that's what you want to do? There is still some time to run on the lease of the apartment."

"I'm not staying in Munich whilst you are working in Holland. What are you going to do, commute back at weekends whilst I'm stuck here during the week looking after George?"

"Okay, I see your point."

"It will cost you a fortune to commute and I thought that we were trying to save money."

"Would you consider moving to Holland?"

"And start all over again! I'd be bored stiff whilst you are working all the time. I've made a few friends here but I don't know anyone in Holland."

"It was just a thought."

"What a mess, here we are renting an apartment in Germany, all of our belongings are in storage in England and now they want you to move to Holland. You couldn't make it up, could you?"

"At least I'm in work."

"True but don't forget that I'm pregnant and have a toddler to look after. We can't just go and put George in storage like a piece of furniture you know."

I could see that Jayne was beginning to get a little upset now which was understandable given our circumstances. I tried to reassure her as best I could.

"Okay, I understand how you're feeling. Things will soon get better; we've just got to stick with it for now."

"I'm sure you're right but why does everything have to be so complicated? I've really enjoyed living here. All I want is a normal family life."

"It's just the way it is at the moment."

"Can't you just get a job back home?"

"I've been looking but you know that my antiquated computing skills aren't in demand like they once were. It's strange that here they are paying 'top dollar' for us and yet there doesn't appear to be any other work around. I think that we should just carry on as best we can and continue to 'milk it' for as long as possible."

I knew that Jayne understood what I was saying but there was no denying that our situation was a little uncomfortable to say the least.

"Look, I'll phone Mum tomorrow and see if she is able to put us up. There's plenty of room in her house so I don't see a problem. Mind you, I don' know how she is going to cope with a small child in the house again after all these years."

"At least it's an option. We will need to decide where we want to live soon."

"I know, it's a difficult one, remember that we need to consider George now. He'll be two in a few months' time and we need to be thinking about schools."

"Yes, I know. Once you are back in the UK, you'll be able to keep an eye on the property market. Hopefully we will see something that we like."

***

It was tough travelling with Jayne and George to Munich airport on the S-Bahn. Neither of us knew what the future held but we were excited about moving back home near our family and friends. Unfortunately for me that meant that I had to continue commuting for the duration of my contract.

One good thing to come out of this was that I would now be able to book a direct flight to Heathrow and wouldn't have to change at either Birmingham or Manchester to fly up to Edinburgh. This was going to save me a lot of time and money.

Jayne's flight was to Birmingham where she was going to be met by my brother Alexander who had kindly offered to take them to Jayne parents' house. This was really appreciated as travelling whilst pregnant with a small child can be extremely stressful, especially as she also had a large amount of luggage.

It was with great sadness that I said farewell to Jayne and George at Munich airport. I'd really enjoyed being a family again and was disappointed that this phase of our life had come to an end.

***

I hated living alone in the apartment. It was nice enough and although it was in a good location, I found it very depressing. It was really lonely without Jayne and George being with me. It wasn't my home anymore; it was just somewhere to sleep.

I contacted the letting agent and told him that it looked

like I would have to leave the apartment a little early. He said that I would have to continue to pay my rent for the full six-months of the contract which I had to 'take on the chin'. He told me everything that I needed to do and was pretty sure that he would be able to re-let the apartment.

I spent several evenings cleaning every part of the apartment. It was hard work but I really wanted to get my deposit back. It reminded me of an Army 'bull night' where you have to clean everything for an inspection the next day.

It was 5 o'clock in the morning when I closed the apartment door for the last time. I put the keys though the post box and that was that. I met Craig at the airport and we waited to catch the first KLM flight to Schiphol.

Craig and I checked into the motel which was located near to the distribution centre. It made sense to stay there initially before we could sort out some more suitable accommodation. The rooms were very basic but we just left our bags there before we went to the work in our new location.

*

The project kick-off party had served its purpose as we'd got to know a lot of people who we would be working with.

The project leader invited me into his office,

"Welcome to Holland Harry, I appreciate that you have been through a bit of an upheaval."

"That's okay. It's good to be here."

"Have you got any accommodation sorted yet?"

"No, we've just checked into the motel down the road."

"Well, I'm sure that you should be able to negotiate a decent rate, especially as it looks like you're going to be here for six months."

"Really, I hadn't thought about that."

"There is a lot of work to be done."

"That's why I'm here."

"We have decided that due to the upheaval you've gone through we thought that we would increase your rate of pay."

"That's very kind of you."

"How does a 10% increase sound?"

"That sounds rather generous, thanks."

"Good, I take it you are working through the same agency as everyone else?"

"No, as you know I was an employee of the company in Scotland so I was able to go direct."

"Good for you. What is your hourly rate?"

I told him.

"So, if we add 10% to that and then convert it into Dutch Guilders, I make it this. Does that sound right to you?"

He'd worked this out in his head and I quickly agreed with his figure. I left the office with my head spinning I couldn't quite believe that I'd just been given a 10% pay rise when if anything I thought that I would have had a pay cut.

Munich is an expensive place to live so I was hoping that I would be able to save some money by working in Holland but now I would be earning more, I couldn't believe my luck.

***

It was late on a Friday evening, Craig and Zaki had gone back to the UK so I was alone in the office. The project leader walked in, he enquired as to how things were going and was very polite and professional but it became clear to me that he wanted results and he wanted them quickly.

I wasn't sure what the reason was and just I assumed that he had his deadlines to meet which was understandable. He indicated that that I could work as many hours as I wanted which included weekends. This wasn't a charitable gesture; it was a little more forceful than that.

I had nothing planned for the weekend so working the extra hours seemed the logical thing to do. He bid me farewell and I sat there alone in the office taking in what he had said.

One advantage of being alone was that there were no distractions, I continued to work for a few more hours and then decided to call it a day. Looking out of the window I could see the traffic on the busy A15 motorway in the distance. This motorway formed part of the European Autoroute (E31) that ran from Rotterdam into the heart of Europe.

It wasn't the best location for me to be working at as it was very remote and I didn't have a car. It was a huge warehouse/distribution centre which required good road communication links and it certainly had that.

I realised that I was in a new phase of my life. It made sense to take what was on offer. I was now earning 10% more than I was in Munich with unlimited overtime. I was away from my family so I might as well go along with things and 'milk it' for as long as I could. It was also a nice feeling that I wasn't working through an agency who would be taking their slice of my earnings.

It was very late when I walked out of the building. It was freezing cold with a bitter wind coming from the east. I put my hood up and walked very carefully along the road towards the motel.

Being located on the outskirts of the town there weren't many facilities nearby such as pubs, shops and restaurants. It was fortunate that the motel had its own restaurant so I made my way over to it hoping to get a nice meal. Outside the restaurant there was a four-foot high wooden model of a windmill which I thought was a nice touch. I ended up having a solitary meal before retiring to my room where I read my book a while.

***

The next morning, I went for a run first thing. I had a rough idea where the town centre was so I made my way there. There was a strong, cold wind behind me as I ran along. It was all very quiet and peaceful but a little slippy underfoot. In the end I turned back as it was just too cold.

I had my breakfast in the motel and made my way to work. The wind was blowing in my face this time and I leaned into it as I slowly made my way along the road.

I showed my badge to the security guard who was sat at the main reception desk. He nodded at me as he knew that I was going to be working over the weekend.

Making my way to my desk I realised that food was going to be an issue. There were some vending machines that sold chocolate and crisps but there wasn't anywhere to get anything substantial.

I realised that I had a good opportunity to learn a lot more about the new computer language so I got to work and tried out various things. Anything I didn't understand I jotted down so that I could ask Craig when he returned on Monday.

It was very late when I walked out of the building but I felt that I'd had a good day and learnt a lot which I thought would be useful as the project progressed.

It was still extremely cold and I gingerly made my way back to the motel. I still couldn't get over how windy it was but thinking about it, Holland doesn't have much in the way of geographical features such as hills and mountains so there is nothing to shelter you from the cutting wind which felt as if it was coming straight from Siberia.

***

The next morning, I went for breakfast again in the motel but this time I secretly pinched some rolls for my lunch as I thought it would be better than eating crisps and chocolate like I'd done the previous day.

I had another good day trying different things out on the computer system and building up my knowledge. It was a bit lonely as I was the only one in the office part of the building with the exception of the security guards who patrolled every now and again.

***

On Monday morning the office filled up with people arriving at different times. The boss asked me how I got on and I told him that I'd made some good progress and had some questions for Craig when he arrived back from Scotland. He seemed to like this and didn't enquire how many hours I'd worked over the weekend.

I didn't have much interaction with anyone so I just carried on doing my own thing. I was pleased when Craig and Zaki arrived back from the UK. We went for a coffee together and had a good old 'catch up'.

I felt that there was a bond growing between the three of us as. Although we were at the heart of the project, we were not in control of what was going on and had very little input into the decisions that were being made. It was still early days but a new pattern of working was being established where we expected to behave in a subservient manner.

***

Jayne settled in at her parents' house as best she could. She enjoyed being with her family and as soon as the 'word got out' that she was back she started to get lots of old friends visit although she soon realised that George was the main attraction.

We had no idea how long she was going to be staying there but we made out that it would only be for a short while until we got ourselves sorted.

We found it really difficult to try and decide what sort of house we wanted to buy and we and more importantly where we wanted to live. We were constantly asking each other questions like,

"Should it be near my parents?"

"Should it be near your parents?"

"What about schools?"

"Should it be near a train station?"

The list was endless and we couldn't make up our

minds about anything. The housing market was very depressed and I knew that as we were cash buyers, we were in a very strong negotiating position but we'd lost money on the last two houses that we'd owned which made us very cautious.

***

The weekend arrived and I was pleased to be going home. The project leader kindly offered to give Craig and me a lift to Schiphol airport which saved a lot of hassle.

I soon realised that it was a lot cheaper to fly from Schiphol to Heathrow than it was from Munich. Obviously, it was a shorter distance but there were more airlines flying that route which meant greater competition.

The bit of the journey I hated most was travelling from Heathrow to Milton Keynes. The tube took about 50 minutes to get to Euston railway station and then it was the same again on the train.

There were other options like hiring a car or getting a coach but hiring a car was expensive and the coach although good value for money they tended to run every two hours so there was a lot of hanging around.

Travelling back on a Friday evening meant that it wasn't fair to ask Jayne to pick me up. The traffic was just horrendous so in the end I just settled for the tube and the train.

*

It was good seeing lots of our family and friends at the weekend but I did find it extremely tiring. It was understandable that Jayne wanted to go out on the Saturday night as she had been looking after George all week but all I wanted to do was flop in front of the TV.

***

CHAPTER 10:

THE NEW 'NORMAL'.

I continued to only fly back to the UK every other weekend. This was partly to save money but also to earn money as I would work when I was in Holland. There was no shortage of work to be done on the project.

It seemed that the more work we did the more that needed to be done. Something new seemed to be added to the list every day. The tasks were divided up between Craig, Zaki and myself, all three of us were working flat out trying to get as much done as quickly as possible.

It was a very intense way of working and it was relentless, but we just kept on working. We weren't involved in any analysis, decision making or design. We just had an ever-growing lists of computer programming tasks that needed to be done.

In the hierarchy of IT teams, I often feel that the programmers are at the bottom, we are often the last to find out about changes and yet have to be the first ones to resolve or build new things.

So many times, something that hadn't even been considered only a day earlier now became our number one priority. It was extremely stressful and challenging working under these conditions and life was very uncomfortable.

*

The project team seemed to grow in numbers each week

and we needed more room to house everybody but unfortunately, there wasn't enough office space available. One day we were led out to a mezzanine area in the actual warehouse. This was just used for ad hoc pallet storage and wasn't part of the main warehouse operations.

They'd made a space for us and had laid out some nice carpet underneath a neat row of desks. There were six tall metal cabinets, one at each corner of the 'virtual office' and two in the middle of each of the long lengths of the rectangular carpet.

There was a row of windows that gave us a good view of the flat countryside and a glass screen that separated us from the main warehouse which was being fitted out at the time.

It was bizarre, as it was a complete office with everything we needed, except that is was in a huge open warehouse. I didn't like the noise that the forklift truck drivers made every so often as they deposited or picked up some pallets but apart from that it worked very well.

*

The EMEA (Europe, Middle-East and Africa) region consisted of different countries across the three continents. Each country had its own headquarters in its respective country. This was normally but not always the capital city. We were to roll the project out to each individual country. The rate was impressive as we would be putting a country live every two weeks.

The first country to 'go-live' was Holland whose headquarters was located in the city of Gouda and we all went there for a visit. The IT manager was a young chap who I'd met before when I worked in Scotland. He was keen for the project to be a success and helped us out as much as he could.

*

The system went 'live' in Holland over the weekend but we quickly realised that there was a problem. Never being shy of coming forward, the managers quickly arranged a conference call with Craig and Zaki who were back in the UK at the time.

We were in a small office and they were both phoned up using two desk phones. Once connected they were both put on 'loud speaker' mode and placed next to each other. It was 'surreal' as we all listened to Craig and Zaki have an in-depth conversation over the two phones but it worked.

We kind of knew where the problem resided but we didn't have the time to fix it over the weekend, so we decided to back out and restore the system to its original state. This was a tough decision but, in my mind, it clearly was the right one.

On Monday we quickly fixed the problem. The core system had a log file and the first record (control record) in this file was a numeric counter. This record hadn't been updated correctly as new records were being added to the file.

The error was a simple oversight but the failure to identify this issue cost us a lot of time plus a little credibility. I expected some blame to come our way but this didn't happen, all the energy was put into fixing this issue. However, in the back of my mind I couldn't help thinking that the issue just shouldn't have arisen. It seemed to me that there hadn't been enough 'end to end' testing otherwise it would have been identified and rectified prior to 'go live'.

*

We successfully went live the following weekend which was a great achievement. However, there were a few issues that we needed to sort out and working on these meant that we had less time to prepare for the next countries 'go-live' which was only two weeks away.

***

For one reason or another Jayne was finding it a little stressful living with her parents and to be fair, George did demand a lot of attention so to give Jayne's mum a break she moved in with my parents in Bletchley. My parent's house was not as large as Jayne's parents but there were two spare bedrooms so it was comfortable enough.

I don't know if my mum had a premonition many years earlier but she'd decided to keep all of our old matchbox and dinky toy cars that I used to play with along with my brothers. These were kept in an old carboard box in the conservatory which soon became George's play room.

One weekend I was looking at George playing with these old cars. He was having a great time in his own little world lining them up in neat rows and making small convoys which he drove around the room. It bought back some lovely memories of my own childhood.

I picked up one of my favourite cars and when I looked at it, I noticed that one of its black rubber tires was missing. This really annoyed me as I thought that George must have lost it whilst he'd been playing. These cars had been played with for years and I really wanted him to respect them.

I looked in the cardboard box to see if it was there and at the bottom, I found several black tires so I thought that these must have somehow come off whilst the cars were in the box. I picked one up and looked at it. It had come apart so there was no way that it could be used again. When I looked at it a bit more closely, I could see that the rubber had perished. I thought that perhaps keeping these cars in the conservatory was not the best idea as it could get very hot in there, especially when it had the sun on it.

George loved that conservatory and he used to proudly show me what he'd made with the plastic bricks whenever I came home. Life wasn't perfect but it wasn't too bad. My mum loved having them to stay but I felt that my dad found it a bit tiresome sometimes.

***

We viewed a lot of different properties at different ends of the housing spectrum but nothing seemed to be right for us. Subconsciously we thought that 'we would know it when we saw it" but that just didn't happen.

***

At church one Sunday morning I chatted with an Irish

lady whose son I knew from a long way back.

"Where's your handsome boy today?"

"He's at his grandparents this morning. We are going to pick him up now."

"Have you got his name down for our school yet?"

"No, he's only two years old so there's plenty of time for that."

"I know some people who put their name down as soon as they are born."

"You're joking!"

"No, it's the best school around and demand is very high."

"I know it's a good school because I went there."

"Well you can never do these things too early."

"Okay, thanks for the advice."

"You're welcome Harry and give everyone my love."

*

A few days later Jayne phoned the school secretary.

"Hello, my name is Jayne Roberts and I was wondering if it was possible to put my son's name down for your school."

"Certainly, what is his name and date of birth?"

Jayne supplied this information and then she said,

"Your surname sounds familiar; did your husband attend this school by any chance?"

"Yes, he did. He was there when it first opened. His name is Harry."

"Well I didn't think it was Alexander."

This may have sounded a bit sarcastic but it was intended to be an 'in joke'. My brother Alexander and I did both attend the school (our older brother was at the local grammar school). Alexander is now a Catholic Priest and due to the vows of celibacy he's not allowed to have children.

"You've heard of them then?"

"I remember them very well. I've been here since the school opened."

"That's interesting; we will have another child to register in a few months."

"Congratulations, can I take a note of your phone number and address?"

"Unfortunately, we don't have either at the moment; we are currently nomads but we are looking to buy somewhere soon. We are currently staying with Harry's parents in Bletchley."

"That's okay, if I can have their details for now so at least I have a way of contacting you should I need to but please let me know your new address as soon as you can. We need to consider where you live as part of your application."

"Oh, I see. Where exactly is the catchment area for the school?"

"It's basically the parish of Bletchley but it does extend a little further than most people think. To the north the boundary is Shenley brook."

"Oh, that's interesting."

"Obviously we prefer practicing Catholics so it will help your application if you are 'known to the priests' but I would think that you know them already."

"Yes indeed. Okay, thanks for the advice. We will be in touch in due course."

"You're welcome and good luck."

"Thanks."

Jayne and I spoked on the phone and she informed me about her telephone conversation.

"Yes, I remember her very well. She was lovely lady and I can't believe that she is still there."

"Well, she remembered you and Alexander."

"Everyone remembers Alexander. The issue here is that we cannot be seen to be given any special treatment just because Alexander is a priest."

"Well, we go to church when we can and there isn't much more that we can do, especially with you working away from home."

"That's true but I suppose we need to buy a house in the

Bletchley area which is going to be a challenge as we still don't know what type of house we want."

Jayne was a very positive person and always seemed to see the good points of any house that we looked at. I found this challenging as it is a really big decision and I knew that it was extremely important to look at any house from multiple angles as one day you are going to have to sell it.

***

There was a small restaurant at the distribution centre which made life a lot easier, it also saved me some money as it was very reasonably priced. Craig, Zaki and I were having our lunch there one day when a small group walked in. I recognized one of them from the Scottish factory where I'd worked a year earlier. He'd obviously opted to stay with the company after our factory closed and later transferred to Holland.

His name was Nathan and like me was ex-forces, he was a larger than life character who always seemed to see the funny side of things. We ended up having a 'good old catch-up'. It was fascinating to learn how successful people had been at gaining new employment.

We both talked very enthusiastically and I could see out of the corner of my eye that I was being watched by senior members of our project team but I didn't care.

"I'd heard you'd gone to Munich Harry."

"Yes, I'm working on the SPEED project and they wanted us to relocate here."

"Where are you staying?"

"In the motel at the bottom of the road."

"I know where you mean, is it okay?"

"I would describe it as functional rather than luxurious but it's convenient and I can easily walk to work."

"How long are you going to be here?"

"I don't have a proper contract but I would say another four months or so."

"I'll tell you what. There is a friend of mine who works here, he also relocated from Scotland and has a three bedroomed apartment in town. If you like I could ask him if he wants to rent out a room."

"That sounds very interesting."

"Leave it with me, he's working later today so I'll ask him."

This all sounded very encouraging. It would be a lot nicer than staying in the motel and I could leave my stuff there at weekends which would be a great help.

*

A day or so later Nathan and his friend Duncan came to see me in our 'virtual office'. I hadn't met Duncan before as he'd relocated from the other factory in Scotland. He came across as extremely friendly and said that he had two rooms that he was prepared to rent out.

"That sound's great, if you don't mind, I'd like to bring Craig into the conversation."

I went over to Craig's desk and said,

"One of the guys over there has two rooms to rent out if you are interested?"

"Sure."

Craig came over and we both agreed that we would like to see the rooms.

"No problem. I'm in this evening so you can pop round anytime."

"Okay, we'll do that."

He told us where his apartment was and we said that we'd see him later. This was really good news; he didn't want much money and it would be far better and cheaper than living in the motel. One small issue was that it was at the other side of town so it would be a fair walk each day to and from work but I thought that the exercise would do me good.

*

I decided not to eat in the motel but walked into town instead. It was a pleasant enough walk and I thought about getting something to eat in a bar but ended up getting some food from a small supermarket which I ate as I continued my walk to find Duncan's apartment.

I walked through a very modern housing estate which looked very neat and tidy. The houses and flats looked small but they'd created a nice area in which to live. There were some attractive open spaces which contained some nice play areas for the children.

Duncan's place was in an older part of town but it still looked nice. Eventually, I found his apartment and pressed the intercom.

"Hi Duncan, it's Harry here. I've come to view your rooms."

"Okay Harry, just come up. I'm on the fourth floor."

"Cheers."

The buzzer went, which released the door and I made my way up four flights of stairs. Duncan's apartment was on the top floor.

It was a nice enough apartment and he showed me to a small bedroom at the back which contained a camp bed and a little furniture. It was extremely basic but nice enough. One thing I did like was that it had a balcony that looked out over some other apartment blocks.

"I take it this is the smallest bedroom."

"That's correct Harry."

"I thought that there was another bedroom."

"There is but I've already let that one."

"Really, that was quick. Did you let it to someone from work?"

"Yes, you pal Craig came round straight from work and took it immediately."

"Did he? The cheeky 'so and so', I was the one that introduced him to you and now he's got the better room."

"You snooze you lose Harry."

"Okay, well I'm happy to take this one."

"Good stuff Harry, you can move in anytime."

"That's kind of you. I've already paid for my room at the motel tonight so I'll move in tomorrow if that's okay?"

"Sure, no problem."

I left Duncan to it and started to walk back towards the town centre. I was a little gutted that I'd missed the best room, especially as I'd told Craig about it but there you go. I didn't think Craig would visit so soon.

*

I stopped off at a small bar in town. It wasn't very busy and I sat down at a table with my beer. I was really pleased that I now had somewhere permanent to stay as it would make life a lot more comfortable.

***

One afternoon it came to light that there was a hire car available if anyone wanted it. I asked about insurance and they said that it was covered by the company so I could have it for an evening if I wanted it.

I decided to accept it although I didn't have a clue as to where I would drive it. However, I thought that it would be nice to have a 'set of wheels' to play with even if it was only for one evening.

I sat at my desk and tried to think of a place that I could visit. I thought about Arnhem which was famous as being the final destination for the world war II military operation called 'Market Garden'. Arnhem was 80km away which I thought would take me just over an hour but what would I do when I got there.

I'd been to the Nijmegen before as I'd completed the famous marches when I was in the Army. This had been an amazing event where we marched 40 kilometers each day for 4 days. It had been a great adventure but going there again just didn't appeal, especially in the winter months.

In the end there was only one place that I really wanted to visit and that was where I was stationed when I was in the Army. It was 150 km away which meant it was going to be a long drive but I felt that it just had to be done.

It felt good to be behind the wheel of a nice new shiny car and within minutes I was driving along the motorway. The route was straightforward enough, initially I headed towards Nijmegen, then on to Venlo where I crossed the border into Germany. I passed Bruggen which also had an RAF base although I'd never been to that airfield before.

The roads started to become familiar to me as I drove along, it had been fourteen years since I'd been in this part of the world but it didn't seem to have changed much. Unfortunately, I'd never actually driven along these roads myself as I didn't manage to learn to drive whilst I served in the Army.

I would have loved to have had my own car at the time. It would have made a big difference to my quality of life during my three-year posting (not that I could have afforded one).

I found a place to park down a side street in Wildenrath village and went for a walk. So many memories came flooding back and it felt like yesterday that I was stationed there. Wildenrath wasn't a very big place and it was very quiet as I walked about.

I didn't know what to do with myself so I went into a pub that we used to go to occasionally. There was a large group of RAF chaps playing pool who were being a little noisy but apart from that there weren't many people there.

I ordered a coke and sat down. It was strange not knowing anyone, that was one thing about being in the Army, you were never on your own. I listened to the RAF's banter as they enjoyed their evening but they ignored me. There was no point in striking up a conversation with them as I was an outsider and to ask questions about the camp would have aroused suspicion. It was a military base after all.

Technically I was still a member of Her Majesty's Armed Forces as I was a serving soldier in the Territorial Army. It was a shame that the TA didn't issue me with an Army ID card which is known as a 'MOD 90'. They only issued them when we went on big exercises like 'Crusader' in 1980 or 'Lionheart' in 1984 (which I was part of).

If I'd had my ID card with me then I may have stood a chance of getting on to the base but I would have had to have given them a very good reason for me to be there.

I had been onto the base as a civilian. Six months after I left the Army a friend of mine got married in a church on the base. There were two churches on the base one was Catholic and the other one was Church of England.

Wildenrath was home to the RAF Harrier when I was there. This aircraft was known as the 'Jump Jet' due to its vertical take-off capabilities. In a wartime situation the RAF camps would be targets for the enemy so the Harriers would operate from secret locations. It was my regiments role was to supply communications to these locations.

The harrier didn't have that much of a range so it made sense for them to be nearer the front line (the Iron curtain as Winston Churchill called it) so they relocated from RAF Wildenrath to RAF Gutersloh. This annoyed the 'locals' when they found out that a squadron of Phantom fighter jets were going to be based at Wildenrath. They weren't happy because the Phantom was a lot noisier than the harrier. I remembered seeing the campaign signs as we went about the local area at the time.

Being a soldier on a RAF base wasn't without its tensions. There is a lot of rivalry between the services. The Army referred to the RAF as 'Blue Jobs' and the RAF referred to the Army as 'Brown Jobs' although between themselves, the RAF referred to us as 'Pongos' because wherever the Army went the Pong (smell) goes. Okay lads, it was funny the first time.

I left the pub and made my way back to the car. It seemed a shame to have come all this way and not get to see a bit more of the area, so I decided to drive to Rheindahlen Garrison.

I'd spent two separate detachments at JHQ (Joint Headquarters) at Rheindahlen during my service and enjoyed both of them. It was the main headquarters for BAOR (British Army of the Rhein). The main office building was known as 'the big house' and I'd worked deep down in the basement in the main ComCen

(Communications Centre).

The first time I was there was when Elvis died which caused a lot of sadness amongst the service personnel. At the time I couldn't understand what all the fuss was about as I wasn't an Elvis fan but in my later years, my opinion has changed.

My route took me near the town of Wegburg which had a notorious ring-road. In its day the ring-road was also used as a racing circuit. It was called Grenzlandring but to us it was always known as the 'Wegburg ring'.

Near the camp there were two bars known as Pops and Eddies. They were on opposite sides of the road to each other and were extremely popular with military personnel. As I drove passed, I noticed that one of them was now a Chinese restaurant; my how things had changed.

When I was there, Rheindahlen was an open camp with no main gate. Anyone could just drive into it but now as I approached, I could see that there was a new security fence. I turned right and as soon as I'd done so I could see a new security checkpoint right in front of me. I realised that I couldn't continue into the camp so did a very quick three-point turn and started to head back towards Wildenrath.

*

It was getting late and knew that I had to start the return leg of my journey. It would have been good to have spent a bit more time there but with a heavy heart I headed back towards the Dutch border.

Driving back, I was beginning to feel very tired. I knew that there was no point in fighting it, so I stopped off at a garage, locked my doors, put the seat down and closed my eyes. I laid there thinking about where I was. I had no backup plan; if I was to breakdown, I wouldn't know what to do. Perhaps there was some documentation in the glove compartment but no-one had mentioned it. I decided it was best not to think about it.

I did manage a little nap and felt better for it. Time was getting on so I started the engine and continued my journey.

I arrived back in the early hours of the morning and once I parked the car I went straight to bed and was asleep within seconds.

*

The next morning, I drove to work and returned the keys. It had been a really good trip and it had been nice to do something in the evening that I wanted to do but I was still very tired and knew that it was going to be a long day.

***

CHAPTER 11:

RENTING AGAIN.

It was a buyer's market and although I knew that we were in a strong bargaining position we still didn't know what type of house to buy. We had a really good deposit and I was earning good money but the memory and the pain of the recent period of 15% interest rates that caused the 1980's housing bubble to burst was still fresh in our minds.

We also didn't know how long I was going to be working and living in Holland. The project was still ongoing and there was plenty of work to do. These thoughts made me very cautious. We also didn't know if it would be possible for us to get a mortgage as I was technically self-employed.

Three years earlier, we were desperately trying to sell a house in Milton Keynes and had no luck whatsoever; now we were really having problems trying to buy one.

***

It turned out that Jayne's brother had a ground floor flat in Wellingborough that was empty. He was working in the Middle-East accompanied with his wife and daughter who was just a few weeks older than George. They recently had moved out there to be with him. He was concerned about leaving his home empty and was more than happy for Jayne and George to live there for a short while.

Jayne packed the car and left my parents' house to drive to Wellingborough which was only 20 miles or so away. It was kind of my parents to let them stay with them while we were living this nomadic life-style. I knew that it had been a bit of an upheaval and had caused them a lot of hassle but it was appreciated. I was determined to make it up to them once we were settled in our own home again.

Jayne's brother didn't want any payment as he knew the house would be well looked after. This was very kind of him but I thought that it wasn't right so in the end we paid him.

It made sense for Jayne to register with a new GP but this meant that our new baby would be born in Northampton. We weren't bothered about this but I knew that it would be a little tedious driving there should we be fortunate enough to have purchased a new home in Milton Keynes when the baby was due to arrive.

***

One Saturday afternoon I decided to give Jayne a break from looking after George so I took him to the park. I didn't know Wellingborough very well so I decided to push him along in his buggy and do a bit of exploring. We walked along a busy street where I noticed a corner shop that sold beer but what made this shop different was that it sold 'real-ale' on draught. Now I like Bavarian beer but I love 'real-ale' so I thought that I would pop back later when the shop was open and try it out.

Once we'd had dinner Jayne told me that she'd rented a video tape from a local shop and wanted to watch it after George had gone to bed. I really wanted us to get a baby-sitter and go to the pub but knew that this wasn't going to happen as Jayne was in the later stages of pregnancy and needed her rest.

I asked Jayne if she wanted anything from the shop whilst we watched the movie,

"If you could get me some popcorn, that would be

nice?"

"Okay, I'll see if I can get some."

I managed to get some popcorn and then went to the small corner-shop that I'd seen earlier.

Inside the shop was a small bar that had two traditional beer pumps fastened to the top, each one had a different label advertising the beer that they were selling. I selected the one that I wanted and purchased a plastic 4-pint poly-pin. The chap behind the bar then inserted a big funnel into the plastic poly-pin and pumped the beer straight into it. This took a little time because the frothy beer needed a little time to settle but within a few minutes I had a full polypin of fresh real-ale.

I walked back feeling good, I wasn't bothered about watching the particular movie that Jayne had chosen but at least I would be able to enjoy a fresh pint of really good English ale.

***

We received a letter from our bank. I couldn't understand what it meant but it appeared that a senior manager wanted to arrange a meeting with us. It was strange that the meeting was to be held in one of the nicest office blocks in central Milton Keynes and not at the Bank's branch.

One Saturday morning we went to find the office and to our surprise we found that it was on the top floor. We went up to the reception desk and took a seat whilst waiting to be seen.

Normally banks are extremely busy places but the atmosphere here was extremely quiet and professional, it was as if we were going to see lawyer rather than a bank manager.

A very well-spoken lady appeared out of nowhere,

"Mr. and Mrs. Roberts."

"Yes."

"Thank you for visiting us."

Jayne and I briefly glanced at each other and then we

both stood up and took it in turns to shake her hand.

"Please follow me."

We followed her passed a couple of open plan offices into her office.

"Please make yourself comfortable."

Jayne and I sat down and an assistant walked in and said,

"Would you like a tea or coffee?"

"Tea would be nice thanks."

"And the same for me, we both just take milk thanks."

The assistant turned and left.

"Thanks again for coming in. The reason I've asked you here is because you've banked with us for some time now and we've noticed some changes in your account usage."

I tried to understand what she was getting at. Obviously, my contracting salary had increased the inflows into the account but I was a little suspicious as to what her point was. Perhaps she was an investigator and was fishing for information to ensure that what we were doing was legal.

The tea arrived and we found ourselves sitting in front of a bank manager drinking tea from posh china cups.

"My job is to look after our exclusive clients."

"Excuse me."

"Looking at your account it appears that you have become more successful."

She had obviously noticed the increased influx of funds that had hit our account due to the contracting rate that I was on. I didn't have an agenda for the meeting but felt that if your bank invites you in for a chat then it would be worthwhile attending.

I thought that it would be useful to build up a good relationship with my bank, after all things can quickly change and I may need their help one day.

"We've noticed that you have some direct debits going to various financial institutions each month."

"Yes, we have a few endowment policies which we bought with a view to paying off our mortgage."

"I haven't noticed a mortgage on your account."

"That's because we don't have one."

"Have you paid it off?"

"No, we don't have a mortgage because we don't have a house."

"So why have you still got your endowment policies?"

"We just kept them going as a saving scheme. To be honest there is no way that they will mature and cover the expected amount but there is a terminal bonus which I thought would be useful."

"But there is no guarantee what the terminal bonus will be."

"True, but in the scheme of things it isn't a lot of money to pay out each month so we thought we would just let them roll along and we can always cash them in should we need to."

"Okay, that makes sense."

I was wondering if her intention was to try and sell us some new policies. I would have pushed back on this as I now knew that the vendors of these policies took their fees out 'up front' so they weren't bothered how they performed over the long term.

One of our endowment policies was equity based. It was our most expensive policy but after seven years it wasn't worth what we had paid into it. The cost to us was £41.47 a month which is £500 a year making our total contribution around three and a half thousand pounds but its current value was nowhere near that.

"We do have one policy that isn't 'with profits' but we've still kept it running."

"Do you have the details?"

"Yes, here they are."

"We have a financial consultant who can look at that for you if you like?"

I looked at her and said, "Okay."

She took the details and walked out of the office. When she returned, I continued,

"I'm really disappointed with this policy, it is very expensive and yet we are losing money on it. It would have been a lot better off if we hadn't taken out this policy."

She didn't make any comment and then a young man entered the room with a beautiful colour print out of the policy. He thought that it was a good policy and recommended that we stay with it.

"But it hasn't even broken even yet and that's after seven years."

"But it's still got a long time to run."

"The units you are buying are sure to increase in value."

"I don't want them to increase in value."

"Excuse me."

"Well if they increase in value now, then that means that I purchase less each month. I want them as low as possible at the moment but as high as possible when I sell. My problem is that I cannot see them going up in value at any time soon."

"There are no guarantees."

"That's true but if we had used that money to pay off the mortgage, we would now be a lot better off, I mean the policy hasn't increase by 15% per annum and yet that's what the interest rate was for a time."

I was disappointed that he was endorsing a policy that I now thought was a load of crap but I was happy that he didn't try and sell me a new one. Well, we didn't have a mortgage so there was no point.

The bank manager continued,

"So, if you don't own a house, where are you living now?"

"We're currently living in Jayne's brothers flat. We would like to buy but don't think we would qualify for a mortgage due to my temporary employment status.

Her eyes lit up when I said this.

"Are you looking for a mortgage?"

"It's in the back of our minds. Do you think we would qualify for one?"

"If you want a mortgage; I can get you a mortgage."

I looked at her a little bewildered. We wanted to buy a house but I hadn't actually looked into obtaining a mortgage let alone apply for one. I realised that this was a mistake, there was no point in house hunting if I was going to be refused a mortgage.

"How much do you think I could borrow?"

"That obviously depends on different factors but you have a good track record with us and are currently earning decent salary, so as long as it's reasonable I'm sure we will be able to accommodate you."

"We're living well within our means at the moment so as you can see from our bank accounts, we have a good deposit."

"Obviously the larger the deposit you have, the better it is as far as we are concerned. It means less risk to us if you are prepared to use your own money."

"Okay, thanks very much for that. We now have options which we didn't have before."

"You're very welcome. If that's it then thanks again for popping in."

"Thank you."

Jayne and I were politely ushered out of the office, we both couldn't believe what we had just experienced. It seemed that we had just 'gone up in the world' without actually doing anything. It was a really good feeling but we both wondered what the catch was.

"I guess that we can look at buying a house more seriously now" said Jayne as we walked along.

"I must admit it's great that we now know that we can get a mortgage but I'm still very nervous about borrowing. I mean, look what happened last time?"

"I know what you are saying but prices are a lot lower now and interest rates appears to be continuing their downward trend."

"The problem is uncertainty; we don't know how long the work is going to last."

This was the big dilemma that Jayne and I faced. It made sense for us to think about buying a family home but at what cost? I was extremely wary of risk. I didn't want to borrow too much; in fact, I didn't want to borrow anything at all but we needed to live somewhere so we decided register with a few estate agents.

We found it difficult to find a house that 'grabbed us'. Obviously, we were in the market for a family home but the new houses seemed too small and it was difficult to find a larger house in a good area that was affordable.

We'd been advised to put George's name down for the school that we wanted him to go to so it made sense to look at houses in that area. Ideally, we wanted something within walking distance.

We went through a lot of pain looking at houses. Jayne arranged for me to view any promising ones when I returned home at weekends, this was the last thing I wanted to do but I knew that I had no choice.

*****

Jayne answered the phone,

"Hello, can I speak to Mr. Roberts please?"

"He's not here at the moment, can I ask who's calling?"

"It's Northamptonshire police."

"Okay, can I help? I'm Mrs. Roberts."

"Yes, it's about your car."

"Our car?"

"Yes, the maroon Vauxhall Astra."

"We do own a car like that. What's the problem?"

"The problem is that it's been stolen."

"Don't be silly, its parked outside. I parked it there myself only last night."

"I think you'll find that it's no longer there."

"Do you mind if I check?"

"Not at all."

"Okay, just give me a moment."

Jayne put the phone down and went outside. She went to where she'd parked the car and then quickly went back inside the apartment.

"You're right, it's not there."

"Like I said, it's been stolen."

"Well, where is it?"

"Can I just check some details with you first?"

"Yes."

"Could you give me the registration number of your car, your full name and date of birth, plus the same for your husband?"

Jayne supplied all the information they asked for.

"Right, your car is parked at this location and you can go and collect it. Unfortunately, it's been 'hot-wired', so your keys won't work."

"So, what do I have to do to pick it up? Will I have to send a recovery vehicle?"

"Will your husband be back soon?"

"No, he works abroad."

"It's not up to me to say what you have to do but it should be possible to start the engine the same way that the thieves did. A mechanic could do this or someone mechanically minded. This would save the cost of a recovery vehicle. Do you know anything about cars?"

"I know how to drive them but that's about it. I don't know anything about the mechanics but my brother knows about electronics and things, perhaps he could help?"

"It's up to you madam but I would recover it sooner rather than later."

"Okay, I'll give him a call. Is there anything else you need from me?"

"No, everything else is in order."

"Before you go, can I ask how you managed to find me?"

"Ah, that wasn't very straightforward. Your car is registered to an address in Scotland, so an officer visited your address but no-one answered the door."

"That's because our house is empty. All of our stuff is in storage at the moment."

"Well, a neighbour told the officer that you were friends with a couple who lived up the street so the officer visited them. They gave the phone number of Mr. Robert's parents. We contacted them and they gave us your parents number who in turn gave us this number."

"Wow, that's a good piece of detective work."

"We try our best."

"Well, I'm impressed."

"I take it your husband is away with the military?"

"Err, no. Why would you say that?"

"Because there was a letter in the glove compartment addressed to Sergeant Roberts."

"Oh, I see. Harry used to be in the regular Army but he's in the TA now, although he hasn't attended for a year or so."

"It's interesting how much information you can find out about someone."

"I suppose it is. Is there anything else you need?"

"No, but I would suggest that you try and be a bit more security conscious in the future. Thieves like it easy."

"Was our car easy to break into then?"

"Not particularly, I understand that you are near Wellingborough station?"

"Yes."

"We suspect that the perpetrator got off the train and rather than get a cab they decided to steal your car."

"Really!"

"It's not the first time that this has happened on your estate. If I were you, I'd think about getting a steering lock."

"That's a good idea officer, thank you so much for everything you've done."

"You're welcome."

Jayne contacted her brother who came over

straightaway. He then took Jayne to retrieve our car which was parked exactly where they said it was. He quickly touched two wires together and got the car started.

"Wow, so it's as easy as that", said Jayne.

"Yes. Now you drive back carefully and whatever you do, don't stall it or we will have to do this again. I will be behind you all the way."

"Okay."

They got back safely and Jayne contacted a mobile machinic to come out and repaired the car so that the key would work again."

***

Jayne and I visited a couple of houses but weren't impressed with what we saw. The prices were okay but they both needed a lot of work doing to them. We didn't have the time or the energy to 'do up' a house, we wanted something that we could move straight into with minimum effort.

Chatting in the car I said to Jayne,

"Do you remember when we came down from Scotland one time; we went and looked at a new show-house on Oldbrook?"

"Yes, it was very near the flat where you were living when I met you."

"That's right and can you remember the prices?"

"They were astronomical."

"At the time they were and that was only a few years ago."

"I feel sorry for anyone who paid those prices, they must be in serious negative equity now."

"They must be; it was strange that they wanted so much for new-builds."

"I can remember at the time thinking that we may not be able to afford to move back 'down south'."

"You and me both. It's amazing how the market has changed."

"And it happened so quickly. One-minute prices were

going up quicker than you could imagine and then next moment you couldn't sell for love or money."

"Well, it's in our favour at the moment so we need to make the most of it and get the right house for the right price that doesn't need a lot of money spent on it to make it habitable."

***

We looked at a 1920's semi-detached house that was located at the western edge of Bletchley. It was in a quiet cul-de-sac which I liked and was convenient for the school that we had put George's name down for. It was a good solid house with a large kitchen that had been enhanced with a single-story extension. The garden was a really good size but needed a lot of work. I was a little concerned about the railway line being nearby but knew that it was only used for freight trains.

The price was okay at over £50,000 and I thought that it would be a safe bet. It needed a fair bit of work but nothing too serious. We tried to negotiate with the agent but we didn't seem to get anywhere. It took a while but eventually we came to the conclusion that there were other forces in play.

We felt that we were being used to expedite someone else's transaction by putting pressure on an existing purchaser to 'get a move on'. We will never know for sure but in the end, we just gave up on the deal which was a real shame but there was nothing else we could do.

*

We were shown a very interesting house which wasn't far from Bletchley town centre. It was an area that I wasn't particularly fond of but the house was immaculate. It was a semi but the thing that surprised us was that they had converted the loft into a spacious office. This really appealed to me and I was pleased that Jayne liked it too.

We put in an offer which was accepted and things were proceeding nicely until we got the survey back. There was a concern that the chimney in the living room wasn't properly being supported. Our solicitor advised us not to proceed with the purchase until it was established that it was okay.

We didn't know what to do. We were running out of time to buy a house and get it ready for our 'new arrival' but I didn't want to end up buying someone else's problems.

The advice that I was given years ago was still in the back of my mind 'remember that whatever house you buy you will want to sell one day so make sure it is a saleable property'.

Our indecisiveness cost us dearly, as someone else sneaked in and bought the house. I was a bit bewildered about the whole process but didn't blame the vendor as he just wanted to sell it.

The strange twist to this story is that many years later I bumped into a chap who I grew up with. He apologised to me for stealing the house. I said that I wasn't worried about it but asked him about the chimney stack. He said that it was still standing and they hadn't done anything to it.

***

We viewed a three bedroomed detached property which was on the busy entrance road to an estate at the edge of Bletchley. It was larger than the property that we sold in Milton Keynes just a few years earlier to the relocation company so if we went for it then at least we could say that we'd moved up the property ladder albeit slightly.

It wasn't the grandest house in the world but I liked it a lot; it had a single garage that was connected to the main house by a carport. The rooms were larger than a lot of new-builds and it had an en-suite off the master bedroom. It had been on the market for some time and the price had been reduced.

We gave it some thought and put in a very cheeky offer. The negotiations went on for some time but we stuck to our guns. We didn't have another house that we were interested in but we made out that we did. In the end they agreed. From my point of view, it was a bargain, we had bought at the bottom of the house-price cycle and couldn't believe our luck.

The price was £75,000 and we contacted our new bank manager to ask if the mortgage was still available. She was surprised that we only wanted to borrow £30,000 but I was still thinking cautiously. We could easily have bought a bigger house and borrowed a lot more.

***

CHAPTER 12:

SHORT EASTER BREAK.

I'd booked my Easter flights well in advance. I thought that they would be more expensive over the holiday period but this didn't appear to be the case. This was a pleasant surprise which I put it down to the competition on the Heathrow - Schiphol route.

There wasn't any letup in the project work that we were doing so we just got on with it as best we could. As Easter approached, I was looking forward to a four-day break. Jayne was settled in her brother's flat in Wellingborough and I thought that we would have a relaxing few days, which would do us all the 'world of good'.

We had a small team meeting where were discussing our outstanding work when it came to light that they expected us to work on Good Friday. I couldn't understand why they would expect this knowing that the three programmers were all based in the UK.

I was really annoyed; it hadn't occurred to me that they wouldn't give us the bank holiday off. I hadn't asked for the day off and just assumed that like Christmas it was a 'given'.

I found out that Good Friday isn't a bank holiday in Holland so everyone would be working. I lost my Thursday flight and had to book another one for the Friday. This was more expensive but I just had to put it down to 'experience' and thought that it would be covered by the extra day's pay that I was going to get.

It was really annoying that my four-day weekend had now been reduced to a three-day weekend.

It just seemed expected that we would work all the hours that they wanted us to. I thought about asking about summer holidays but the emphasis was always on the project's immediate objectives.

***

Leaving the distribution centre on Maundy Thursday I started to walk back to the apartment. I was fed up as I knew that the Easter weekend was starting in the UK and here I was, stuck in Holland on my own.

Rather than go to the apartment I decided to head into the town and have a bite to eat. Later on, I was sat alone in a Dutch bar. I'd had a few drinks and was contemplating things.

It was April 1994 and I reflected on the fact that I was still entered into the London marathon which was just over two weeks away. I'd deferred my entry from the previous year because of all the upheaval of my redundancy and my move to Munich.

Under the rules you are only allowed to defer your entry once. This was to allow runners who became injured to run the following year. Getting into the London Marathon is a bit of a lottery and the temptation to run with an injury could cause a more serious problem so it was a very sensible rule.

The fact of the matter was that I could either run the race or not. It was just a simple case of 'use it or lose it'.

The biggest problem was that the marathon was so close and I hadn't properly prepared for it. I'd gone out for the odd run here and there but that was about it. I'd tried for years to get accepted into 'the London' and had completed it two years previously but I'd trained very hard for that race.

I was annoyed with myself for not thinking about it

sooner but the project had become just so overwhelming that all I'd being doing was working. I sipped my beer and the voice in my head asked,

"Do you think you could do this Harry?"

I didn't know the answer but I did know that if I didn't turn up then it would be years before I would be accepted to do the race again. I knew that the week before the marathon was the 'wind down' week, that meant that I only actually had ten days to do any serious running.

"TEN DAYS, TEN DAYS!" I kept saying to myself.

It was a crazy situation but I only had myself to blame. If I'd only thought about it sooner and done a bit more training, I would easily have been able to complete the course but now I just didn't know.

***

My Dutch colleagues were in good spirits but I hated being in the office on Good Friday. To me it was such an unnatural thing to do. We'd endured a harsh winter and now that the weather was a bit better it would have been nice to have some time off with my family.

***

Once I got to Heathrow, I took the tube to Kings Cross and walked to St. Pancras station using an underground walkway.

I made my way into the awesome railway station with its huge curved roof. To me it was extremely impressive but looking around I was very disappointed at the state it was in. It was filthy and very badly maintained. There was litter everywhere but most disappointing thing for me was the lack of trains to Wellingborough.

Here I was on a Friday evening, tired and exhausted. All I wanted to do was to get home but I had to wait nearly two hours for a train. I couldn't believe it. I knew it was late but I didn't expect train problems even if it was a bank holiday.

I bought my ticket and went back into the main station. I was really annoyed with everything and couldn't understand why travelling home was so difficult on public transport.

I didn't know what to do with myself so I decided to go for a walk. My route took me away from the busy area and although there weren't many people about, I began to think that perhaps this wasn't such a good idea.

Once I made my way back to the station, I looked around for a pub. There didn't seem to be much choice but eventually I found one and went in. There were not many drinkers there which surprised me but this wasn't a normal Friday, this was Good Friday.

I was quietly enjoying my pint when suddenly they rang the bell 'Last orders please'. I couldn't work it out. Here I was in London, one of the greatest capital cities in the world and the bar was shutting early on a Friday night. When I asked at the bar the Irish girl said,

"It's Good Friday and pubs shut at 10:30 on Good Friday."

I believed her but still found it hard to take in. How could this be the case? I finished my drink and made my way back to the filthy St. Pancras station.

I eventually made it to Wellingborough and walked the short distance to the flat. I was pleased to see that our car was parked in the small carpark nearby. I was very tired and irritated due to my long journey so I went to bed straightaway.

*

The next morning, I went out for a run before breakfast. I didn't know Wellingborough very well so I just ran wherever I fancied. If I was running a regular route, I would have known exactly how fit I was because I would have been able to compare my time with previous runs. This would have given me a good indication of my fitness level which in turn would help me in my decision as to whether to run the marathon or not.

There was a big landmark and I decided to head towards it. I didn't know anything about the industrial history of the town but it was a huge water tower that had 'Leyland' painted on it in white with a blue background. I assumed that this meant British Leyland so I figured that there must have been a factory that made car components there at some stage.

It was hillier than I thought but obviously it made sense to put a water tower on high ground. I hated running on the road so I decided to turn back and ended up following the river which had the biggest swarm of swans I'd ever seen.

I was pleased with my run and when I got back to the apartment, I did lots of stretches. Jayne thought that I was mad even considering running a marathon without having completed a proper training program.

"But if I don't do it this year, I may never get the chance again."

"But you haven't done the training."

"I know but I'm not in bad shape and what's the worst that can happen? If it's too much for me I'll just stop and catch the 'tube' to the finish and collect my stuff."

I could tell that Jayne wasn't convinced but she knew me well enough to understand that once I got an idea in my head if was difficult to stop me.

***

The following weekend I remained in Holland. I did a full day's work on the Saturday but instead of walking back to the apartment I changed in to my running kit. I put my jeans and t-shirt into my daysack which I put on and made my way out of the distribution centre.

I ran towards the town centre and stopped for a moment to look at the huge river (Boven-Merwede) that connected Rotterdam with Germany. I was hoping to find a nice towpath to run along but couldn't see one so I ran along a road for a few miles before returning back to the town centre.

I made it back to the apartment and felt really good. The run had gone well and I was very pleased with myself although I knew it wasn't long enough but the good news was that I didn't have any injuries which was the most important thing.

*

On the Friday evening I treated myself to a hire-car from the airport. It was a medium sized model and was really comfortable to drive down the motorway.

The next day we all drove to London; I didn't have a clue as to where I was going to park but I just hoped that I would find somewhere near the Barbican. In the end we found a multi-storey went and registered for the race.

It was a hassle having to go to London to register on the Saturday for the race but I didn't have a choice. It would have been quicker and easier to have done it earlier in the week but that wasn't an option for me.

I was tempted to spend some time in London and see a few sights but I thought that this would be very tiring so we drove back home had pasta for dinner.

*

The race went okay on the Sunday. I took it steady and kept to the same pace for nearly the whole race.

I was tired at the end and finished in around 4hrs 45 minutes. Considering my lack of training this was a really good achievement but I was angry. I was angry with myself for not doing better than I'd done only two years previously when I finished in 4hrs and 1 minute.

I think I'd deluded myself that I could improve on my time which was a just ridiculous. There is no short-cut to marathon training. If you want to do well then you have got to put the hours in.

***

The next day I was finding it uncomfortable to walk as I waited for my bags to arrive at the carousel at Schiphol airport. Once I'd cleared 'arrivals', I noticed a couple of smartly dressed chaps who were in the queue at one of the many car-hire booths. I didn't know them but I recognised them as I'd seen them at the distribution centre before.

I assumed that that they were hiring a car to go there so I went over to them,

"Hi, I hope you don't mind me asking but are you by any chance going to the DCE?" I asked.

They both looked at me and one of them said,

"Yes."

"Do you mind if I cadge a lift with you?"

"Not at all."

I couldn't believe my luck; I now had a lift straight to work. This was a godsend to me as it would save my tired legs and I'd get to work a lot quicker than using the train.

We introduced ourselves and were joined by another person, we then made our way to pick up the car. They spoke amongst themselves as we walked along and they made no attempt to bring me into the conversation.

The car was a nice new saloon and the keys were given to the youngest member of the group. He took them enthusiastically and we all made ourselves comfortable. I was sat in the back and just listened to their conversation. I got the feeling that they didn't want me there which I thought was a little rude.

Although the DCE had only been open for a couple of years I knew that the company was having a rethink of its strategy. To assist with this, they had bought in the services of a top business consultancy and these guys all worked for the consultancy.

If I was a consultant working on a project for a client I would try and obtain as much information about the client as possible. This would obviously involve talking to lots of people. I thought that here was an opportunity for them to ask me lots of questions as I'd now worked for the company in three different countries but they didn't ask me a thing so I tuned out of their conversation and let them get on with it.

We arrived at the motorway and immediately the young driver headed straight for the fast lane. He put his foot down and accelerated as fast as he could. I knew that the autobahns in Germany didn't have a speed limit and I assumed that this must be the case in Holland too.

I couldn't believe the speed he was driving. The other two passengers didn't seem bothered at all but I was terrified and angry that the driver was risking our lives and for what, just to save a bit of time.

I sat as low in my seat as I could and mentally practiced the brace position where I would put my arms up to protect my head. My senses were on 'red alert' and I knew that I would only have a second or so to adopt the position should the driver lose control.

I was angry because I thought that my life was in danger and as a married family man, I wasn't happy about it at all but what could I do about it. There was no point in asking them to drop me off on a busy motorway as there was no way I could continue my journey. I just sat there quietly trying to anticipate anything that could lead to an accident.

We eventually arrived at the DCE and once I retrieved my bag from the boot, I thanked them for the lift. One of them just nodded and then walked off with the other two. I followed them into the building and was grateful to be alive. It was good that I got there so quickly but I thought that the whole experience was ridiculous. I didn't know what they were trying to prove and they certainly didn't impress me.

I did see them at the airport the next time I flew in a couple of weeks later but I did my best to avoid eye contact and made my way to the railway station.

***

Once I was back at my desk a few people chatted to me. I don't think they believed that I'd completed the London marathon the previous day although I did show them my medal. They asked me about my time but I just said that I was just happy to enjoy the experience as I knew that I hadn't done enough training.

Apparently if I wanted to do a fast time then I should

have done the Rotterdam marathon as it is a really fast course. I tried to explain that my goal was just to finish the 26.2 miles and that's what I did.

**

It took a couple of months to complete the purchase of our new house and when we went to the bank to sign the mortgage papers, I changed the amount that we were going to borrow. Due to the amount I was earning I was able to reduced it from the originally agreed £30,000 to £20,000. I don't think that they had seen anyone do this before but I was pleased that they allowed us to do this without question, after all they made their money by lending money.

They had a special offer where they would charge us a reduced interest rate for 1 year. This made our new mortgage very affordable, especially as the base rate was slowly coming down. However, I still had my goal of not having a mortgage at all but realised that the mortgage interest rate was now not that much different from our saving rate, well for a year anyway.

The vendor said that we could have the carpets for £1000 but we thought that this was a bit cheeky as we assumed that they were included in the price. This told me that they weren't happy with the agreed purchase price but my view was that they didn't have to accept our offer.

**

Having contributed to England's failure to qualify for the 1994 world cup finals in America. I found it difficult to support the Dutch team although I was living and working in Holland.

The Dutch clearly loved their football, but there wasn't much talk about it in the office, it just wasn't that sort of environment. Everyone was just too busy working to spend much time socialising.

Due to the fact that there were no British teams taking part I took an interest in the Irish team (well my grandmother was Irish) and was amazed how Jack

Charlton managed to do so well with the small talent pool that he had as his disposal. He knew he didn't have the 'superstars' that many teams had. I remember him saying in an interview,

"We don't let other teams play the way they want to play."

I enjoyed the world cup; it was a very welcome distraction from the daily drudgery that was my normal life. I watched a few games in the apartment and a few in the pub.

Holland had a good tournament but they eventually succumbed to Brazil who went on to win it. The morning after they lost, the atmosphere in the office was very subdued. Being English, I knew how they were feeling due to the many disappointments we'd had over the years.

It was tempting to gloat but, in the end, I decided to be a little subtler than that. Eventually, I managed to pluck up enough courage (I was tempted to say Dutch courage) and said,

"I don't know guys, you let me down. Here I am working in Holland and I could have said that I was there when Holland won the world cup but unfortunately it wasn't to be."

No-on said anything; they just carried on with what they were doing.

***

One of the German computer programmers from Munich had been temporally assigned to our project. His name was Hermann and I'd first met him when I worked in Scotland a couple of years earlier when he came over for a visit as we needed to work together on a piece of work.

He was a bit surprised when I turned up in Munich. He was some ten years older than me and was a real character. He was a permanent employee and refused to work weekends and with German employment laws being what they are, there was nothing that they could do about it but somehow, they managed to relocate him to Holland.

I was envious, he seemed to have employment rights that 'us contractors' didn't have; my impression was that we were there to be 'used and abused'. I originally thought that he was Bavarian but this turned out not to be the case.

Originally the plan was for him to fly in from Munich every Monday morning and return on a Friday. However, he put it to them that he would prefer to drive. At nearly five hundred miles each way, this was one hell of a long 'commute'.

My understanding was that he could claim a generous mileage allowance. He had an old but reliable car and he didn't appear bothered at 'clocking up' around a thousand miles each week. I thought that it was madness but it was only going to be for a short while, so why not make a bit of money out of it.

*

I was sat at my desk in Holland working away and my phone started to ring. This was unusual as I didn't get many calls so I gingerly picked it up.

"Hello, Harry speaking."

"Hi, is that Harry Roberts?"

"Yes, speaking."

The caller had a distinctive Scottish accent and I recognised him immediately but was a little shocked that he was calling me. He wasn't from the Scottish factory; he was from the Territorial Army unit that I'd served with in Scotland.

"Hello Sir, this is a surprise. What can I do for you?"

"I'll tell you what, you took some finding."

I remembered that for some reason I'd left them the phone number of the company's European headquarters in Munich. He'd obviously phoned there first and eventually had managed to track me down.

"I'm sorry about that. Anyway, what can I do for you?"

"I'm afraid that it's not good news, we haven't seen you for over a year now and unfortunately that means that you are no longer a member of the TA."

It took a moment for this to 'sink in'.

"Are you still there?"

"Err, yes. Sorry about that."

"The thing is now we need you to return your kit."

"Okay, but unfortunately it's all in storage at the moment but we are about to move into a house in Milton Keynes. Unfortunately, I can't see me going back to Scotland anytime soon."

"Okay, could you please take it to the TA Centre in Bletchley when you can?"

"Yes, I could do that."

"Good, I'll let them know so that they will be expecting you."

"Okay, that's fine."

"Good, take care now."

He then hung-up. I continued to hold the receiver in my hand for a moment and then slowly replaced it in its cradle. I was in shock. For the first time in eleven years I was now no longer a soldier.

I felt that people were watching me so I got up and walked towards the toilet but instead I made my way to the stairwell which was covered with a glass arch.

I looked out of the window at the countryside and could see the motorway a short distance away. I knew that not turning up for any TA training for over a year was not ideal and I knew that I should have at least been in contact with them but to kick me out without any warning was a bit harsh.

I was 'gutted', the TA had been a really big part of my life and now it was no more. I was now officially a civvie. It was all over, that was it.

I felt sad but understood their reasons. I went and got a cup of tea and as I made my way back to my desk, I just kept thinking,

"Eleven years, eleven years."

Then another thought came to me; Eleven years' service in the Territorial Army was a good achievement but to qualify for the TA medal you had to do twelve. I was one year short.

"BASTARD..."

***

Hermann could see that something was troubling me and said,

"Hey Harry; Craig and I are having a meal in the motel tonight. You are welcome to join us if you want to?"

I thought about it for a moment. The motel food was okay, it had a good grill and obviously I'd got to know the staff who were friendly enough.

"Do you know what Hermann? I don't mind if I do."

*

Afterwork the three of us made our way to the motel. There was a little green painted wooden model windmill outside which I always thought was a really nice touch as it was a good reminder that we were in Holland.

"Are you okay Harry? I saw that you received a phone call today."

"Umm... Yes, I've had a little bit of a shock. The phone call was from the Admin officer of the Territorial Army unit that I'm part of in Scotland. Unfortunately, because I haven't been there for over a year, they have kicked me out."

"Did you not know about this?"

"Well obviously I knew that I hadn't turned up for over a year but what with working away from home and all the hours that we've been doing there wasn't much I could do about it."

"I've never understood why you joined the Army in the first place. The UK does not have 'Wehrpflicht' or conscription like we do in Germany."

"There weren't many options for me when I left school and I thought that it would be a bit of an adventure. Anyway, I thought that the Germans could opt out of National Service if they wanted to."

"Our conscription is for eighteen months but it is not

compulsory. You can opt out if you are a conscientious objector or have medical issues that prevent you from serving."

I knew that the German Army had an excellent reputation but I also felt that young Germans didn't want to be associated with Germany's military past. Hermann didn't give anything away but I suspect that he didn't do his National Service. A soldier can easily spot another soldier and I didn't get that 'vibe' from him.

"What's the point of having conscription if it's not compulsory?"

"Germany has changed a lot since the second world war. No-one wants to live in a dictatorship again. We are a prosperous peaceful country now but we are still very aware of our military history."

I was a little concerned where the conversation was going. The last thing I wanted to do was offend Hermann but looked me straight in the eye and continued,

"The thing is Harry; you need to remember that we are very good at playing 'zee bad guys'."

***

CHAPTER 13:

HOME AT LAST.

Once the house purchase had been completed at midday on the Friday, Jayne had to go on her own to pick the keys up from the estate agent. It was an exciting time for us, it also formally concluded our little Scottish sojourn. We were now back home.

It's always a big job moving house but Jayne had to do it on her own with added burden of having George to look after and not forgetting that she was pregnant too. I was a bit wary of letting her do all this and told her repeatedly not to overdo things. Later in the evening we spoke on the phone.

"So, you're in then?"

"Yes, and guess what?"

"What?"

"You remember that we refused to buy the carpets. Well, they've taken the lot."

"What all of them?"

"Yes, every single one. We're looking at bare floorboards throughout."

"Crickey, that must have been a horrible job taking all them up."

"Well they've done it. I'm not sure what they will do with them but they aren't here."

"I suppose they were within their rights to do this but I've never heard of it before. I think that they must still be angry at the price we paid for the house."

"But they didn't have to accept our offer, did they?"

"True. Anyway, what are your plans now?"

"I'm going to clean everywhere and see if I can get some carpets fitted. I'm just so pleased that we haven't agreed a date to get all of our stuff out of storage yet. It will have to stay there a little bit longer as there's no point in getting it all delivered until the carpets are down."

"Okay, are you staying there tonight?"

"Yes, I've made a small bed up for George and me."

"Okay, well have a good night and give George a kiss from me."

"Will do, love you."

"Love you too."

I was disappointed about the carpets but we just had to get on with it. It would have been great to have been flying home this weekend to help out but I was needed to support another country's 'go-live'. It was another event where I was to man the phones in Holland whilst the team were on site at one of the subsidiary countries.

***

Once the carpets were down, Jayne organised for all of our belongs to come out of storage. One day a big lorry arrived and the men set to work unloading everything. It was a big job deciding where everything had to go but Jayne managed it all brilliantly.

It was really exciting for George as he now had his own bedroom. He was delighted to rediscover some of his favourite toys that he hadn't seen for eight months.

Any boxes that Jayne thought that we didn't need immediately were put up in the loft out of the way. Some of these boxes are still there and haven't been opened for more than 25 years.

***

It was a great feeling flying back to England for the weekend knowing that for the first time in months I would be going to my own home. I'd only been in the house two times before and that was when we viewed the property.

Growing up I remembered that there was a really big local debate about where to build London's third airport. One of the sites was only about 20 miles from Milton Keynes. I like many local people was against this but now I thought that perhaps it may have been a good idea as it would have made my commute a lot easier.

There were a few different sites that were considered and I remembered that one of the rebel's slogans was, "Yardley Chase is not the place" which I thought was rather clever.

It was a great feeling waking up in my own bed in my own house. It was really early and no-one else was up, so I got my running kit on stepped outside the house.

I made my way towards Shenley brook which I remembered from my childhood. In those days it was in beautiful countryside but now it ran between various housing estates as it made its journey towards Furzton lake which used to be called 'Denbigh pit'.

The planners had done a fantastic job landscaping the brook and it was a real pleasure to run along in the fresh morning air.

My destination was Howe Park wood which is a lovely ancient wood that had been preserved for people to enjoy. It took me a little while to find it as I wasn't familiar with the route through what is now the Tattenhoe housing estate. When I got there, it was a pure joy running through the wood as it was just so peaceful.

Running back, I was happy that we'd bought in a good area. Every so often I came across a small park and thought that we would spend many a happy hour playing with George and 'one other' which did indeed prove to be the case.

***

Time was passing very quickly and I informed my team leader that I would soon require some time off as Jayne's pregnancy was nearing 'end of term'. He was completely indifferent to my request and wouldn't commit to anything. I knew that there was an awful lot of work going on but surely, they could cope without me for a few days.

I didn't know what to do as he hadn't given my guidance at all. I needed to know what my boundaries were. Could I work from home, or couldn't I? I certainly didn't want to be in Holland when the call came through that Jayne had gone into labour. There would be no way that I could fly home in time.

Jayne was extremely upset when I told her,

"This is ridiculous, they've got to let you home surely?"

"I just don't know what to do, they're not giving me any guidance at all."

"I can't believe it, after all you've done for them. Remember the complications we had when George was born. I need you here, I can't go through this on my own."

"Okay, I understand. Really I do."

I tried to calm Jayne down as best I could but it was a tricky situation. They needed to 'cut me some slack' somehow. I thought that it was morally wrong not to make allowances for me in this situation. I told them when I first moved to Holland that my wife was expecting so it wasn't as if they didn't know.

I got the impression that my team leader had been given direction from 'above' and I remembered overhearing a conversation once where he was told,

"You've got to push, push, push and push…"

Everyone was working long hours and there was obviously a lot of pressure to achieve results. This was an opportunity for a few people to make a name for themselves in the company. To be associated with a successful project would definitely be good for their careers.

There was little or no HR involvement in the project and there was nowhere I could go to get some help and advice. I'd often thought that our European cousins had extensive employment rules and regulations. Well if they did, then they didn't seem to apply to us.

My personal situation and previous life experiences didn't help me cope with the huge amount of work that they were putting on me. Having served in the Army I was well used to being 'put upon'. The Army is all about discipline and hierarchy and I often found it difficult to be assertive when it came to standing my ground.

Being a self-employed contractor, I had little or no support. There was no holiday entitlement, no sick pay, no HR department to go and see. If I wasn't in the office then I wasn't getting paid, it was as simple as that.

I felt extremely insecure, this job was all I had, there was no other work out there that I could find. Oh, how I envied people with regular jobs and normal lives.

*

I realised that the only way I could guarantee that I would be at the birth was if I went AWOL (Absent With Out Leave). This would be an extreme course of action but they couldn't say that I hadn't warned them. I wasn't in breach of contract because I didn't have one, well a written one anyway.

If I didn't show up for work then I wondered what they would do about it. They would obviously try and phone me to find out what was going on but I could easily ignore their calls. In the end I realised that there was nothing that they could do other than tell me not to come back when I eventually made contact.

I felt that this course of action would jeopardize my position but what was I supposed to do? My wife needed me and she needed me now. There shouldn't be any debate about it, I needed to be at my child's birth.

***

Previously I'd been envious of contractors. They were extremely well paid and were often regarded as a valuable business resource. Looking at the cars in a company's car park once, I noticed that all the expensive cars were either owned by either senior managers or contractors. Becoming a contractor was one way of bypassing the slow climb up the business hierarchy to get on a good wage.

The project team had been growing but the new team members all seemed to work at the edges of the project. They weren't 'hard core' programmers who could roll up their sleeves and get stuck into some complex computer programming. They seemed to be business analysts or specialists in specific areas. I often wondered if they were all really needed but one thing was sure and that was that the Dutch company that placed them would be making a tidy profit out of it.

I found the micromanagement completely overpowering. I'd been working flat out in Holland for nearly six-months. I'd worked extremely long days and every other weekend. The weekends that I wasn't working were tiring for me too because I had to fly back to the UK and then when I got there, I became Dad.

***

When George was born in Scotland, there were some unexpected complications. Obviously, we wanted things to be better this time so we explained everything that had happened to the midwife. We were relieved when we were informed a bit later that the hospital had opted for a 'planned birth'.

This was really helpful to me as I could now inform my manager of the exact dates that I would be off work. However, when I told him, he was completely nonplussed and wouldn't confirm whether I could have the time off or not.

I struggled to accept his attitude. I couldn't believe that anyone could be so inconsiderate. I'd been working all the hours humanly possible and now I needed some time off I couldn't understand why he was making life so difficult for me.

There was no way I was going to miss the birth of my child and I felt really disappointed that they weren't giving me the flexibility I needed. Childbirth isn't a straightforward process that runs to a strict timetable, even with a planned birth. I needed them to give me a bit of flexibility but it just wasn't forthcoming.

Jayne phoned me at work a few days later and informed me that the hospital had set a date for the birth, I immediately went over and told my team leader. He looked at me for a while and then he said that I would be able to work from home for all of that week. This was really good news and I phoned Jayne back immediately.

***

It felt good flying back to the UK knowing that I was going to be there for a whole week. I still had lots of work to do but at least I would be at home. Jayne's mum Lilly had kindly offered to stay with us and look after George whilst Jayne was in hospital. This really was kind of her and took the pressure off us whilst we concentrated on the pending arrival of our second child.

On Saturday morning I found the storage box that contained my old PC. I just hoped that it would still work as it hadn't powered up for several months. If I couldn't get it to work then I would just have to go and buy a new one, this was a purchase that I hoped that I wouldn't have to make.

Jayne had bought a small purpose-built computer desk which was discretely located in the corner of our small dining room. It fitted nicely behind the door and I setup the computer placing the monitor on the top and the PC on the floor. There was a 'pull out' shelf designed for the keyboard. It was perfect for our needs.

I'd bought an external 14,400 Fax Modem which I plugged into the back of the computer and to the telephone socket on the wall. Once everything was connected, I turned the PC on and was relieved when it came to life. Once it was fully 'booted up' I tried to connect to my company's computer network via our normal telephone line.

The modem made some distinctive noises as it 'did its thing' and I waited patiently for my computer to connect to the company's computer network. I keyed in my network password and from there I was able to logon to all the different HP3000 computers that I need to. It was also possible for me to read my emails.

I sent a couple of emails to my work colleagues and also one to my boss just to prove that the system worked and that I was 'on line'. I knew that they wouldn't be happy if I couldn't logon for any reason as that was part of the deal.

That was it, I was all set.

***

My PC was obviously slower than working in the office but it was okay. I could do everything that I wanted to do within a few minutes of logging on and all from the comfort of my own home.

It was going really well until George realised that I was at home. He didn't understand that I didn't want to be disturbed as I worked away in the dining room. He kept banging on the door saying,

"Daddy, Daddy, Daddy."

In the end I had no choice and let him in. He was excited to have me around and who could blame him as it was such a rare occurrence. The trouble was that he kept distracting me so in the end I gave him his own chair, sat him on it and put a spare keyboard on his lap which wasn't connected to anything.

I pressed some keys and I told him to do the same which he did. It was a sweet moment as he typed away and I kept encouraging him saying that what he was doing was really good. He liked the attention but after a while he got a bit bored and went off to get a drink.

***

During the week we told George that he was about to become an 'elder brother' but being two years old he didn't seem bothered about it. We didn't know the sex of our pending new arrival and we weren't bothered if it was going to be a boy or a girl.

***

On Wednesday afternoon I drove Jayne to the hospital and she settled in as best she could. We were both naturally a bit nervous about the operation which was scheduled for the next day but they knew all about Jayne's medical history and seemed confident that everything would be alright.

It was a very emotional saying 'goodbye' to each other. I told her to get as much rest as she could and that I would see her in the morning. Driving home, I was in a little world of my own. I just wanted everything to go well.

***

I got up early and quickly got dressed; it was a really big day in our lives and I wanted to get on with it. It felt strange and exciting that in a few hours I would be meeting a new member of our family for the first time.

George was still asleep so I didn't disturb him. I said goodbye to Jayne's mum and drove off. I didn't know what the restaurant was like at the hospital so I stopped off at a 'trucker's pit stop' which was only a short distance from our house (42 Café).

I tucked into a large traditional fry-up surrounded by builders and workers. I felt a little out of place but that didn't bother me. I just thought that I needed a good breakfast inside me as I didn't know how the day was going to 'pan out'.

There was a lot going around my head as I drove out of Milton Keynes. It was a 'red letter day' but I knew from previous experience that these things were not always as straightforward as you would like.

Jayne was pleased to see me and just wanted the birth over with. I sat down next to her bed and talked about anything I could think of to take her mind of it.

Eventually the time came and Jayne was transferred to a small operating theatre. This time I was allowed to be present but before I could go into the operating theatre I had to 'gown-up' and even had to wear some wooden clogs.

The atmosphere in the operating theatre was very relaxed. Jayne was naturally extremely nervous and I tried to reassure her as best I could.

They put a screen up over her tummy so that I couldn't see what was going on. The surgeons started the operation and didn't hang about. I was tempted to look but thought better of it.

It wasn't long before I could hear our new born baby crying.

***

I arrived back home and felt very tired but also relieved that everything turned out well. Lilly greeted me and I gave George a big hug saying that he now had a little brother. He didn't seem bothered either way and then Lilly turned to me and said,

"How is my daughter and not forgetting my new grandson?"

"They are both doing very well thanks."

"I trust everything went well."

"Umm, it wasn't that straightforward with Jayne being diabetic. She doesn't like not being in control of her sugar levels."

"I can understand that but she's just had a major operation."

"I know but you know what she's like."

"Well she needs to be careful and make sure she doesn't overdo things."

"Yes, well so far so good. They are keeping her in for a few days so hopefully she will be able to get some rest."

"As long as she does, by the way some weasel has been on the phone for you."

"Excuse me?"

"Some chap from Holland wanted to speak to you."

"You're joking."

"No, I explained to him that you weren't available because your wife was giving birth but he was most insistent."

"That's shocking; I told them that this was the day that my child was due to be born."

"Well, I explained that but he didn't seem bothered."

I was starting to get a little angry. How dare they phone me up at home and today of all days? It wasn't right and it showed me how little they cared about my situation. I thought about phoning back but decided against it. They would only give me something to do which was the last thing I wanted.

"Thanks for that Lilly."

"Well, hopefully they won't call back."

"I've got to logon tomorrow morning so I'm sure there will be some urgent emails waiting for me."

"Well, make sure you don't log on tonight. Tomorrow is another day. I've made you some dinner, it's in the kitchen."

"Thanks, you have been a great help. Did George behave himself?"

"He's been very good; he needs something to occupy him and then he just gets on with it."

"That's good, I was a bit worried."

We knew that the new addition to our family would be a big change for George. Up until now he had been the recipient of all of our love and attention without even trying. Now, whether he liked it or not he was going to have a rival. This concerned us but we weren't aware of anything we could do about it and thought he would just have to accept the situation and get on with it, after all he's not the first child in the world to have a new brother or sister.

Someone mentioned that they had similar concerns when their second child was due to arrive and I remembered them saying,

"The arrival of a younger sibling is in effect the start of a new relationship."

"Okay."

"Normally you have a choice about who you have relationships with but not in the case of siblings. They are effectively 'stuck with each other'. It is therefore essential that this new relationship gets off to a good start."

"So how do you do that?"

"What we did was we bought a present for our eldest child. We had it all wrapped up and kept it hidden away and when we introduced our new baby to the our eldest, we give him the present saying that it was from his new baby sister."

"And did he fall for it?"

"Not really, but a present is a present and he felt good about it and that's what we wanted."

*

Jayne and I spent some time thinking about what would be a good present to get George from our new baby. We wanted it to be a large present so it would be memorable but we also didn't want it to be too expensive.

In the end we decided to get George a large multi-coloured plastic toy truck which Jayne duly wrapped up and kept hidden in the bedroom wardrobe.

*

I went up to our bedroom and got the toy truck from the wardrobe and put it into a large holdall bag that also contained some things that Jayne wanted me to get for her. Walking down the stairs I realised that George was in the living room watching a cartoon on the TV so I was able to go out of the house, put the bag in the back of the car and sneak back in without him noticing.

I really wanted to sit down and relax in front of the TV but I knew that I had to go back and visit Jayne again. This time I took George with me and also went and picked up my parents who were very excited to see their new grandson. Unfortunately, I couldn't fit Lilly in the car but she decided to leave it for now and would visit Jayne the next day.

***

It was lovely introducing George to his new baby brother. He wasn't sure what was going on and seemed a little confused but he loved getting the present.

Jayne was relieved that it was all over but she was also very tired. We didn't stay very long and left her to get some rest. It was fortunate that she didn't have to do any feeds as our second child was being cared for in SCBU (Special Care Baby Unit).

I dropped my parents off and took George home. Lilly was watching some TV so I got George ready for bed. He proudly showed his Grandma his new truck and I let him play with it for a little while before tucking him up in bed and reading him a story.

It had been a momentous day and I was so grateful that Jayne and our new baby were okay. It was a bit daunting as I now realised that we had two children to look after but I tried to put that to the back of my mind. For the time being I extremely pleased with the arrival of our new son Joseph.

***

Craig decided that he wanted his own place and rented a small cottage which wasn't too far away from the distribution centre. He stayed there alone for a little while and then his girlfriend joined him.

Now that there was a spare room in Duncan's apartment, I decided to ask him if it would be okay for Jayne, George and Joseph to stay for a short holiday. He was okay about it and agreed straightaway so I decided to be a little pushy and said,

"Is it okay if they stay for five weeks?"
He looked at me and said,
"Okay, but I hope your children aren't too noisy."
"Well, I cannot guarantee that they will be angels,
George is only two and Joseph is two months."

I was really pleased with his kind and helpful attitude. It meant a lot to me and I'm sure that Jayne would again produce some really good food in the evening. I don't know why he was so obliging; perhaps he just fancied a bit more company.

Having Jayne and the boys staying with me was really good news, it lifted my spirits knowing that my growing family were going to be with me again. It also meant less travelling for me which was an added bonus. Staying in Duncan's apartment meant that it would be a lot cheaper than renting my own place and it would also be a lot less hassle too.

***

CHAPTER 14:

MAKING THE MOST OF IT.

I picked up Craig's phone,

"Good morning, Harry speaking."

"Hi Harry, it's Clive. How are you doing?"

"Oh, hi Clive. I'm doing fine thanks, how are you?"

"You know, 'same old, same old'..."

Clive was also a contract computer programmer who was based in Munich. He was a really nice chap and I had a lot of time for him.

"I was after Craig, is he there?"

"I'm afraid that he's not here at the moment but I'll get him to phone you when he comes back, if that's okay?"

"That would be great, thanks."

"So, what's new in Munich?"

"I guess the big news is that there is a huge project kicking off. It's starting in America and they are looking to replace ASK's ManMan computer system with Oracle Financials."

"Wow, that is a big move."

"It sure is. Obviously, the decision's been made at the company's HQ in America."

"I know that the ManMan system is a bit old now and there is a lot of uncertainty about the support but we've changed it so much that they don't support us anyway."

"Well, keep it under your hat for now Harry. I'm sure it

will be public knowledge soon enough. Anyway, when are you guys coming back to Munich?"

"I'll tell you what mate, I'd move back tomorrow if I could. We are being so micromanaged here that it wouldn't surprise me if we have to 'clock in' and 'clock out' every time we go to the toilet soon. We are just so busy that there's no time to think about anything."

"I get that impression. I guess that's why they wanted to transfer you all up there."

"Tell me about it. There is just no let up, the work just keeps on coming."

"Okay, Harry. It's been good talking to you and take care now."

"Cheers Clive, speak to you later."

I put the phone down very slowly. This conversation was a 'game changer'. If they replaced the core business computer system with Oracle Financials then everything we'd done on this project will have been for nothing. It was a scary and depressing thought.

***

Jayne phoned me at my desk at work.

"There's a letter for you which looks like it's come from America."

"Really, that could be good news."

"Why, were you expecting it then?"

"Well yes; kind of."

"What do you mean?"

"Well, I'm hoping it might be a cheque."

"A cheque! What for?"

"Why don't you just open it?"

The phone line went quiet whilst Jayne opened the envelope.

"Oh my God, it is a cheque."

"That's great; it's the profit from selling my shares. I faxed them the details but I had no way of knowing if they were going to process it in time."

"Wow, you kept that quiet."

"I didn't know if I was going to get it or not and I didn't see any point of getting your hopes up."

"Do you know what? This would cover the cost of the new three-piece suite that we need for the living room."

"Really?"

"Yes, come on; you know we need one so we might as well treat ourselves. It's a bonus after all."

"Okay, we'll talk about it when I'm next home."

"Great. I'll start looking."

*

We did indeed go and purchase a new three-piece suite and very comfortable it was too. In fact, I would go as far as saying that it was the most comfortable sofa that I'd ever sat on but maybe that was because it was a freebee.

***

Jayne was delighted when she found out that she could stay for five weeks and immediately set to work planning things. One thing that needed to be sorted out was Joseph's baptism. We were lucky because yet again, my brother volunteered to conduct the service. He gave us some dates when he was available and Jayne soon came up with a plan,

"If we have the baptism on this particular Saturday then we can all drive to Holland on the Sunday."

"Okay, that works for me. So, you're happy for me to book the overnight ferry from Harwich to the Hook of Holland?"

"Yes, but please make sure you get a cabin. I know what you are like, anything to save a few quid."

"I don't know what you mean," I said sarcastically.

"When we dock in Holland, how long will it take to drive to where you are working?"

"I would guess that it will take about a couple of hours. It should be a good drive because the roads are really good. They chose the location of the distribution centre because of its proximity to the Rotterdam docks the road links into Europe."

"That's good. It also means that once you drop us off at your mate's apartment on the Monday morning, you can then go straight to work. That will mean that you won't upset your boss by taking some additional time off which I know he doesn't like."

"Indeed. If you're happy then I'll book a flight home for the Friday and a return ferry for the Sunday evening, complete with a four-birth cabin."

"That will be perfect. There is one other thing."

"What's that?"

"I'm going to invite as many members of our family as I can to Joseph's baptism, this means that there will be a lot of children attending so I thought I would book a bouncy castle."

"A bouncy castle! At our house; where on earth are you going to put it?"

Our back garden was on different levels. The previous owners loved gardening and had created some very large flower beds which were contained by a complex pattern of low brick walls. These were of different heights and looked beautiful but it didn't work for us with young children, especially as George just wanted to run around.

"How about the front garden?", said Jayne.

"I guess it would just about fit there but would they be able to put it up on the slight slope?"

"I can ask them but I don't see why not."

"Okay then, you can have a bouncy castle."

"Great, leave it with me."

I felt a lot happier when I put the phone down. Things were beginning to get better for me. I'd be living with my family again, albeit for a short while. I'd save time and money by not travelling back to the UK every other weekend which I found very tedious and tiring.

*

Friday came and I was given a lift to Schiphol. I was excited about the weekend ahead of me which I knew was going to be 'full on'. One thing was for sure; Joseph's baptism was going to be completely different from George's due to the large number of family and friends that we had invited.

George was baptised in Scotland in a lovely church in pretty little place called Tillicoultry which was three miles from where we lived in Dollar. We were able to use the services of my brother Alexander who was visiting us at the time.

The parish priest kindly let us 'do our own thing' in his church one weekday evening. This was very kind of him but it meant that we were the only people there when George was baptised. This didn't create the best atmosphere and we really missed not having our family with us.

When I got to Heathrow, I took the tube to Euston station and then took the overland train to Bletchley. It wasn't the quickest route home but there were plenty of trains which meant that there wasn't much waiting around.

When I arrived home, everything seemed to be well organised. How Jayne managed to pack everything for a trip to Holland, organize a baptism which was to be followed by a party at our house complete with two young children was beyond me. I figured that she could cope better when I wasn't around distracting her and getting her way.

The next morning, I quickly realised that I was Dad again as George demanded my attention. It was nice that he was excited that I was home but I didn't have time to play with him as we had to get ready.

There was a knock at the door and I opened it to meet the man who was delivering our 'bouncy castle'. He rolled it out quickly in the front garden and it fitted perfectly. He pegged it down securely with some huge metal stakes and then blew it up to make sure it was functioning properly.

He let it down straightway much to George's disappointment as he wanted to get on it and have a good bounce around. I was a little nervous leaving it there in its deflated state whilst we attended the service but felt sure that our kind neighbours would keep an eye on it.

We all got dressed in our smart clothes and made our way to 'All Saints' church in Bletchley. Jayne's family weren't Catholic but they were all very keen to support us which was lovely.

I got a buzz watching everyone arrive at the church. There were some family members there who we hadn't seen for a long time, some of whom had travelled a long way to attend which was very much appreciated.

We had the whole church to ourselves but this time there must have been around a hundred guests in attendance which made for a great atmosphere. I really appreciated the effort that everyone had gone to.

Alexander conducted a very dignified service and it all went very well. He created a lovely warm atmosphere and everyone relaxed and enjoyed the occasion. I know Alexander is my brother but I'm still very proud of him. Speaking in public is something that horrifies me even to this day, but he always seemed to make it look so easy.

*

When we got back to our house it was bedlam trying to get everyone a drink. My dad kept on at me,

"Gin and tonic for your mum, gin and tonic for your mum…"

I knew that mum would be patient enough. I could see that she was enjoying herself chatting to her sister but dad was being a bit of a pain. I served the drinks a quickly as I could and when I dished them out, I said that everyone could go and help themselves next time.

The bouncy castle was a big hit with the children who also encouraged a few adults to join in. I watched my dad struggle to walk on it whilst trying to help George. It was clear that George didn't need any help and was more capable than my dad but it was fun to watch.

There was a bit of a queue for the toilet so I nipped upstairs into our bedroom and used our en-suite. I was a little taken aback when Lena started shouting out,

"We know what you're doing. We know what you're doing..."

I turned around and when I looked out of the window, there she was bouncing higher than I thought humanly possible. So much for discretely going to the toilet. I shouted out of the window,

"You shouldn't be looking."

*

Later in the day, when things had quietened down a bit, I decided it was time for me to treat some of our guests to a nice malt whisky from my collection that I'd been slowly building up on my travels to and from the continent.

There were a small handful of guests who 'were up for it'. We found a quiet spot away from the noisy children and arranged some chairs into a small circle. Once everyone was settled, I gave everyone a nice crystal whisky glass.

Looking in one of the cupboards of our lovely welsh dress I produced a nice bottle of Macallan single malt. This is one of my favourite whiskies and I thought it would be perfect to share with everyone.

Once everyone had a 'tot', one of my guests said,

"I think that this calls for a toast."

"Good idea."

He then stood up and said,

"Ladies and Gentlemen. It's good to see you all here on the auspicious occasion and I'd be grateful if you could all be upstanding."

Everyone stood up.

"I'd like to propose a toast to Joseph."

We all raised their glasses and said,

"To Joseph."

Everyone took a sip of their whisky and then we all sat down and continued to chat amongst ourselves. The conversation flowed and one whisky led to another as I knew it would.

I always enjoyed these family 'bonding moments' but unfortunately, I began to get a little carried away and decided to open a bottle of cask strength Glenmorangie.

This was 60% proof whisky and from a financial point of view this wasn't a good move as deep down I felt that this bottle of whisky was going to be worth a lot of money one day as it had an individual serial number. At that moment in time I didn't care about its monetary value. I was having a good time surrounded by my loved ones and I felt that we all deserved a bit of treat, so why not?

Once everyone had finished their whiskies and I opened the bottle. The first thing that 'blew me away' was the aroma. This was the 'real deal' and 'blew the socks off' everything else that we'd drunk previously.

I poured a small amount into each glass and we all savoured the glorious smell before gently sipping it. My Dad was so 'into the moment' that he rushed off to find my mum. When they both came back my dad gave his glass to my mum,

"Try that," he said insistently.

I could see that my mum couldn't quite see what all the fuss was about but she slowly raised the glass to her mouth to take a sip. We all watched her intensely to see her reaction. She slowly tilted the glass back but just before she got to taste it my dad grabbed the glass from her hand and shouted,

"Don't gulp it!"

We were all shocked as she hadn't even tasted it, let alone gulped it.

"I'll tell you what mum, I'll get you your own glass."

When I returned with a glass, I could see that my dad was a little bit embarrassed with his outburst but nothing more was said about it. However, the phrase "Don't gulp it" has now became a bit of a catch phrase in our house and we still use it today. It brings back fond memories.

*

The 'banter' continued and someone said that we

should give our small group a name. Lots of ideas were thrown around which was rather silly and amusing too.

In the end we settled for "Drinking Relatives Exclusive Gathering Society" or DREGS for short.

***

The next morning, I slowly opened my eyes and quickly shut them again. The sunlight pierced into my eyeballs like a javelin hitting its target. We had a big day ahead of us and I'd clearly overdone the drinking yesterday.

Jayne got everything organised as usual and before I knew it, we were racing toward Harwich for the ferry to the Hook of Holland. We were late and Jayne drove as fast as she could. There was no way I was able to drive so I was pleased that she was happy to get behind the wheel.

I felt a little sad when I looked at the ferry as we waited to drive on board. It would have been nice if we were going on a family holiday rather than taking my family on what could be described as a business trip.

If anyone deserved a holiday then it was us. Our quality of life was just awful, we were living apart and I was only seeing Jayne and the boys every other weekend. I was working flat-out earning as much as I could whilst I could. It felt like all I did was work and sleep but deep down I knew that it was for the greater good as I still believed that security is 'money in the bank'.

I'd booked a cabin for the overnight sailing and the next day I felt okay to drive to Gorinchem. When we got there, Duncan's apartment was empty so I showed Jayne where everything was. I then left her to it and drove to work.

I worked a little late to make my hours up but once all the managers had left, I quickly made my way to the car park. I got into my car and drove the short distance to the apartment. It felt strange being in a car, it gave me an element of freedom that I didn't know that I'd missed.

Opening the apartment door was brilliant. The first thing that hit me was the smell. Jayne had clearly been working her magic in the kitchen and as I was taking this in George came up to me 'on the run' and gave me one of the biggest hugs I'd ever had.

We had a lovely family meal and Duncan joined us later. I then found myself in the 'bath-bottle-bed' routine again. Joseph settled down very quickly but George was being a bit of a pain so I tucked him up in bed and read him a story. Once he looked like he was going to go to sleep I joined Jayne in the living room and we opened a bottle of wine.

***

Duncan refused to accept any extra payment from me for Jayne and the boys to stay in his apartment. Yet again I was experiencing the generosity of the Scots. He had a television which was really good as the Dutch channels didn't dub the actor's voices so we were able to understand what was being said when an English or American program was on. They also had the two BBC channels so it felt like we were at home.

Jayne had bought some of George's favourite videos to watch but obviously he couldn't watch them without a video player.

"I wouldn't have packed them if I'd known that there wasn't a video player."

"Sorry, I forgot to mention that."

"It's just that they take up a lot of space and are quite heavy."

"I know but it's a lot nicer staying here than in some boring hotel. Believe me its far better than the motel where I stayed when I first started working here."

*

I took George out for a walk one evening to burn off some energy. We soon came across a small park which he loved. We explored a bit more and I spotted a small group of children and their parents who were gathered near a small fence. We went over to see what they were doing.

There was a small paddock that contained a variety of

different animals including sheep, goats and baby deer. The families were feeding them with their meal leftovers. It was a lovely scene, excited children and proud parents, a real family moment.

George was fascinated by the animals but we didn't have anything to feed them so we looked around for some long grass. One of the mums kindly gave George some carrot tops and he pushed one through the wire fence. A goat quickly tugged it out of his hand and he jumped back a little startled. I thought that this would 'dent his confidence' but he quickly recovered and pushed another carrot top through the fence.

He loved feeding the animals and this was to become our 'evening routine' for the next few weeks whilst we stayed in the apartment.

***

I'd visited Holland on a school trip. We stayed at a coastal resort called 'Noordwijk ann zee'. It was a lovely trip and I distinctly remembered visiting a theme park for the day. I couldn't remember what it was called so I asked some of my Dutch colleagues if they were aware of it. They all seemed to think that it was a place called 'Elfteling'.

Elfteling is a fantasy-themed amusement park so there are a lot of attractions based on ancient myths. I found it on the map and thought that it would be a good family day-out.

We set off early one Saturday morning. I was getting used to driving in Europe and I would say that I found it less stressful than driving in England. We found it easily enough and were soon enjoying walking around the lovely fairy-tale forest. George found the statues fascinating and we never knew what we were going to find next as we explored the park.

We had a lovely family day out and I would really have liked to have the Sunday off but as usual, I needed to go to work.

***

The implementation schedule of the new IT system was very aggressive. It meant that we had a country 'go-live' every two weeks or so. No two countries were the same and we had no choice but to cater for their individual needs. These individual requirements were categorised into 'must haves' which needed to be completed prior to go-live (show stopper), and less important requirements that they could 'live without' for a short period of time.

I'd worked on implementations before but normally after go-live there is a period of consolidation where things settle down. This was not the case on this project as no sooner had one country gone live then we had to work on the preparation of the next one. It was extremely stressful as our priorities kept changing all the time.

For the three of us it was relentless. We were never able to 'take a break' and the pressure was constant. I kept waiting for a 'let up' but it just never came.

I was constantly thinking about programming and even when I was relaxing my subconscious mind was working on how I was going to fix a bug or figure out how I was going to overcome one issue or another.

The one thing I hated was when I was writing some code and was just getting 'into it' someone would come over and say,

"Stop working on that. You need to do this as it is more important."

I understood that there was a list of priorities but couldn't understand why they kept on changing all the time. We were supposed to adapt our minds to meeting these requirements in an instant. I struggled with this; my head seemed to be spinning all the time.

On many occasions I thought that they should just leave me alone to finish something because I was in 'the zone' and very near to the completion of something. I knew that it would take me longer to 'get back into it' than it would to just carry on and just finish it.

One downside to this way of working was that I became wary of putting lots of effort into a specific task because I felt that they would ask me to stop working on it at any moment.

*

Having my family around me was great. I really enjoyed being together. George demanded my attention all the time but this helped me forget about work for a moment anyway. I loved taking him to feed the animals each evening; it was a special father and son moment.

One evening we were out shopping and I decided to purchase a video recorder. I thought that it would help entertain George which would make life a little easier for Jayne during the day.

*

I was a little disappointed that I wasn't involved in any of the project implementations. These were done 'on-site' and it would have been nice to have been able to do a bit of travelling but obviously not whilst Jayne was here.

Craig was asked to go to Copenhagen for a weekend which he was really excited about but rather than fly there he decided to drive and take his fiancé. I was a little envious as it looked to me like it was going to be a bit of an adventure. This turned out to be the case as he didn't realise that he had to take two ferries.

When different countries went live, I always seemed to be in the office taking calls and trying to answer questions. It was depressing and I often felt very lonely as I always seemed to be the only member of the project team around.

Jayne didn't like me working long hours during the week or at the weekend and she had a point. She was trying to make the best of a bad deal but I didn't know what to do about it. The pressure of work was always there, I felt that they just couldn't leave us alone.

I put it to the 'powers that be' that I wanted a weekend off. I explained that my family was here and felt that we deserved some time together. It wasn't a nice experience and I felt that I had to grovel. Jayne wasn't happy either saying,

"In a normal working environment, if a company wants an employee to work over the weekend, they would have to ask you. There is such a thing as employee rights. Here they expect you to work all the hours God sends and if you want a weekend off you have to 'suck up to them'."

"It's just the way it is at the moment, especially with all the 'go-lives' and all the changes that we have to make. It's the demands of the project."

"Demands of the project! Well, if this project is so demanding then perhaps, they should staff it accordingly and not treat their staff this way. What's wrong with employing more people?"

"They have been trying but they can't seem to get anyone with the right skills who are available at the moment."

"Well, they should slow things down a little then. It's ridiculous expecting people to work like this."

"I know what you mean but I just don't know what I can do about it at the moment."

***

CHAPTER 15:

WEEKEND TREAT.

I'd enjoyed Elfteling so much that I looked around for something similar. I'd always thought of theme parks as being all about the rides but walking around some lovely grounds watching how much George was enthralled when he discovered new things was a pure delight.

I nipped into a travel agent to make some enquiries. The lady who served me was extremely helpful when I asked about ideas for places that we could visit for a nice weekend treat. Time was precious to us so I wanted to go somewhere nice. In the end I settled for a place that was further away than I would have liked but felt sure that we would have a lovely time.

There was a good choice of different accommodation options and thinking about our situation I decided to go for the most expensive. One of the reasons was its location to the theme park. This hotel was located at the theme parks entrance so we wouldn't have to travel at all once we got there.

The girl processed my booking and I got the feeling that she was a tiny bit envious. I bet she wondered who this Englishman was who was working in Holland spending a lot of money on a lovely weekend. I would normally have gone for the cheapest option but not this time, this time we were going to have the best.

I told Jayne that I'd got the weekend 'sorted'.

"You haven't told me where we are going yet."

"To be honest I didn't have a clue when I went into the travel agents but in the end, I decided that we deserved a treat. Unfortunately, it's a bit of a drive away but I think it will be worth it."

"How far away is it then?"

"About two hundred and seventy-five miles."

"That'll take ages, we'll have to leave early on Friday then and I'm sure your boss won't like that."

"Well, we'll just have to see what happens."

"Anyway, you haven't told me where we are going yet."

"Ah, well. I know that you think I'm a bit of a cheapskate but not this time. This time I've gone for the best."

"How much have you spent then?"

"Around a thousand pounds."

"A thousand pounds! On one weekend! Are you mad?"

"I just thought that we deserved a treat."

"I know but a thousand pounds, just on one weekend is a bit steep to say the least."

"I just thought that whilst we are together, we should make the most of it."

"Okay, but where are we going?"

"We are going to be staying at the Disneyland hotel in Paris."

***

When using the train to commute to and from the airport the train stopped at the city if Delft. From the train you got a really good view of the city because the train track was elevated on a viaduct (which has since been demolished). It looked like a really nice place to visit so I suggested to Jayne that we should go there one Sunday morning.

I knew Delft was famous for its pottery and technology amongst other things but apart from that I didn't know anything else about it.

Walking about we came to the main market square which was huge. At the western side was the Stadhuis (town hall) and at the opposite end was a beautiful church called Nieuwe Church. It was a fantastic open space with lots of people milling about which I assumed were mostly tourists.

We found a spare table at a restaurant which had a covered outside area and ordered two coffees. It was just lovely 'soaking up the atmosphere' but George soon got bored so I ended up chasing him around the square whilst Jayne fed baby Joseph. George was just loving running around and I enjoyed it too.

Once George had calmed down, we went and had a good look around some of the shops selling the famous blue and white pottery called 'Delftware'. In the end, we decided to buy a rectangular ceramic tile which had a pretty picture of a windmill painted on it. It was framed in wood and we thought that it would be a good souvenir of our time in Holland.

We slowly made our way back to the car. It had been a simple family day out but an extremely enjoyable one. It was just great to spend time with my family and forget about work for a while.

***

It was a Friday afternoon and the slight chance of me getting away from work early was fading rapidly. There was a 'panic on' and I needed to fix something before I could leave for the weekend. They didn't care that I wanted to get away, they just wanted the 'fix' completed as soon as possible.

It was nearly seven o'clock before I managed to get to the apartment where Jayne was waiting. She wasn't happy but I assumed that she'd been expecting me to be late. Fortunately, everything was ready so we quickly packed the car and started our long drive to Paris.

We arrived at our destination just before midnight. I drove around the car park looking for a space. Arriving so late had its drawbacks but in the end, I was lucky enough to find one and as I reversed into it, I said to Jayne,

"I'm not so sure that I feel safe parking here."

"Why?"

"Have you seen all the other cars?"

"Yes, what about them?"

"Well, look at them. They are all so posh."

Jayne looked about her and sure enough the carpark was full of luxury cars, all of them appeared to be in immaculate condition and here we were in a 'beat up' old Vauxhall Astra with a dent in the door.

"I think that we need to take extra precautions."

"Harry, what are you going on about."

"Looking around I would say that our car stands out. I think that we need to be extra careful don't you."

Jayne looked at me as if I'd completely 'lost the plot'.

"No, I'm not happy about parking here. I think that we'd better put your new steering lock on just to be safe…"

∗∗∗

The next morning the magic began, we were only there for the weekend so we had to make the most of every second. We started by going down to breakfast but we weren't alone, it didn't take long for us to be joined by various Disney characters who systematically 'worked the room'.

Joseph was oblivious to what was going on but George was enthralled. He'd seen many of the movies which we'd bought on video tape but he didn't realise that the characters were actually real…

∗

We went back to our room to prepare for our trip inside the park. Our hotel was located right above the main entrance so we could see all the guests arriving. It was clear that it was going to get extremely busy so we got our things together and went straight into the park.

Suddenly we were in a different world, there was just so

much to take in and George looked around in bewilderment. The first thing I took him on was a traditional carrousel where he was strapped onto a horse (a bit like the ones in Mary Poppins) and off we went.

We bimbled our way around the park and stopped off at anything that took our fancy. Jayne and I took it in turns taking George on a few gentle rides. We were slowly getting into a new parental routine that allowed us to look after two children.

At lunch time we made our way back to the hotel and it was then that George spotted that there was a swimming pool. He said that he wanted to go swimming. I turned to Jayne,

"Can you believe it? Here we are in a fantastic theme park and George wants to go swimming?"

"Remember he's a child."

"I know that but he can go swimming anytime."

"I've packed our swimming clothes."

"Well it looks like we are going swimming this afternoon then."

I was really against the idea of going swimming but George insisted and to be fair it was his holiday too. The pool was lovely and I was surprised how busy it was.

George loved the water but after a short while he started 'playing up'. I couldn't work out what his problem was and I began to get annoyed because it was his idea to go swimming. He ended up sitting in the small water filled recess where swimmers cleaned their feet when entering the pool area.

He wouldn't move so I grabbed him from under his arms and picked him up. He still wasn't happy and started to scream in my right ear. It was then that I saw it.

Floating in the small pool of water was a small but perfectly formed 'jobbie'.

I couldn't believe what I was looking at. Here we were, in one of the poshest hotels I'd ever been to in my life and my son had just had a crap in the swimming pool. It was time to leave and quickly.

*

We went back to the room where George laid on the bed with a bottle of warm milk. Jayne and I had a cup of tea and we watched TV for a while. It was good to have a rest although I thought that it was a bit of a waste when there was so much to see but I was learning to 'go with the flow' as far as being a parent was concerned.

We ventured back into the park and ended up watching the firework display that we'd missed he previous evening. It was a good finale to the day and then we all went straight to sleep.

The next day we again had the 'character breakfast' and did another quick tour of the park before starting our long drive back to Holland.

We stopped off at a service station and I took George to a small play area whilst Jayne changed Joseph's nappy. George started to climb up an inverted 'U' shaped wooden climbing frame and for some reason I just left him to it and turned my back to go and sit down on a bench.

No sooner had I done this than I heard him scream. I spun round and could see that He'd fallen through the climbing frame. Unfortunately, his head was too big to fit through the gap so he ended up hanging there with his head wedged between two pieces of wood. His arms were outstretched and he continued to scream.

I dashed over to help him but fortunately, another Dad got there first and supported his body. We then pushed him back up through the gap, he then let me lower him to the ground.

I looked at him in disbelief, he was crying his little heart out. Fortunately, he seemed okay. I thanked the other Dad and picked George up and took him to see Jayne. I was in a little shock myself. It was a scary moment that could have ended up a disaster.

We continued our journey but kept a very close eye on George. He was obviously still very upset but didn't show any worrying signs. I was a little angry with myself that I hadn't kept a closer eye on him but it happened in an instant and just as I turned my back.

It was very late when we got back to our apartment. Both the boys were asleep in the car so we carefully carried each one up the stairs and put them straight to bed. I then went back to the car and bought up all of our stuff. Once everything was sorted, we sat down and had a beer. Jayne turned to me and said,

"Thanks for a lovely weekend Harry."

"You're very welcome. I really enjoyed it but I'm still a bit shocked at what happened to George as the service station."

"I know but don't beat yourself up about it."

"It's just that it happened so quickly. I'm so grateful to the other dad who was there to help him."

"Yes, you need a bit of luck sometimes."

"Do you think that we should have taken him to the hospital to get him checked out?"

"He was obviously upset but appeared to be okay. I'm pretty sure that there is no long-lasting damage. He's sound asleep now so we will have to keep a close eye on him tomorrow."

"Okay, but apart from that it was a great weekend."

"Yes, it was nice to be able to treat ourselves."

"Back to work tomorrow, and then we have the long drive back to the UK on Friday."

"It's been really good visit and I'm glad that you come over."

"It was really kind of Duncan to let us stay here."

"Yes, it made all the difference."

"Remember that on Saturday we are going to your Uncle and Auntie's ruby wedding anniversary party."

"Is that on Saturday?"

"Yes, it's in London."

"How are my parents getting there."

"I don't know, I assume that they will go by train. We

can't fit them in our car as we will have the boys with us."

"I'm sure that they will sort something out. Wow, that's going to be a busy weekend. We won't get back home until nearly lunchtime and then we will have to drive to London."

"Just make sure you get some sleep on the Ferry."

"I'll do my best; we can always share the driving."

"That will mean that neither of us can have a drink."

"I think that's appropriate, don't you? After all we now have two very young boys to look after."

"True."

We finished our beers and called it a night. It had been a wonderful family weekend albeit very tiring. I was going to miss them all terribly but at least we had made the most of our short time together.

***

Friday arrived I managed to leave work on time which made a pleasant change. Jayne had written a thank you card for Duncan which she put on the table. In the card she said,

"Thanks for everything Duncan, please find the video recorder instructions and guarantee as we are leaving it here for you to keep."

*

It wasn't long before we were driving towards Rotterdam to get the night ferry from 'the hook of Holland' back to Harwich.

We decided to get something to eat on the ferry rather than retire to our cabin straightaway. There was a canteen style restaurant that allowed us to choose exactly what we wanted to eat which suited us perfectly.

The ferry was extremely busy but we managed to get a table to ourselves. We were all tired but I thought that a good meal would settle everyone done for the night. I turned to Jayne and said,

"This takes me back."

"What do you mean?"

"Travelling on this Ferry, I must have done it a dozen times or more."

"Was that when you were stationed in Germany with the Army?"

"Yes, I used to get the train from Monchengladbach straight to the Hook of Holland and then when the ferry docked at Harwich, I used to get the train to Liverpool Street station in London."

"I've been on this ferry too."

"Really?"

"Yes, my dad and a couple of the boys were working in Germany on the building sites and I went to visit them once."

This was news to me and I listened intently.

"Did you travel alone?"

"Yes, and I ended up getting stuck somewhere but some kind people looked after me."

As Jayne told this story I suddenly had a memory 'flash back', now this may sound extremely implausible but something popped into my head that I'd never thought of since the day it happened.

I didn't say anything because I knew that if I did, it would just sound too ridiculous to be true. Instead I asked her more questions about her trip to see her family in Germany.

"How old were you?"

"Seventeen."

"So, you travelled alone to meet up with your dad and two of your brothers?"

"Yes."

"That sounds very exciting. Were you nervous making that trip?"

"A little, after all I was very young and I was travelling alone so I needed to be careful."

"I bet you did, but you made it in the end."

"Yes, it was good fun."

We finished our meal and made our way back to our

cabin. We tucked the boys up in bed and then crawled into our own bunks. I lay there unable to sleep for a while. I was thinking about Jayne's story about her own journey on the ferry years earlier.

I remembered being on the ferry one time but I couldn't sleep on the seat so I gave up and went for a walk around the ship.

Whilst I walked around, I saw a young girl sitting on her own and she looked extremely nervous. I couldn't tell you what she looked like but what I distinctly remembered was that there was a kind of connection between us. This felt like it was on a spiritual level, my heart went out to her as I somehow knew that she was uncomfortable in her surroundings.

I felt the urge to go over and give her a big hug and tell her that everything was alright but this didn't make any sense because I'd never seen her before. I was dumfounded, what felt so natural to me was so wrong. There was no way I could go up to a stranger and give her a hug.

I was really confused and didn't know what to make of it all and then a voice in my head spoke to me. It was my own voice which said,

"You can't do that Harry; you've got to go round the houses first."

This also didn't make any sense to me but it was as if I'd been given a secret look into the future. The stars weren't aligned in our lives at that point in time but one day they would be.

I remembered that an hour or so later I walked around the ferry again and felt a similar sensation as I walked past her for a second time. I glanced over but she didn't look at me.

It was just so bizarre and defied all logic so I quickly forgot about it until this evening when Jayne told of her experiences. I don't know if that girl was Jayne or not and never will know for sure but I believe it to be true and that's all that matters.

***

We arrived back at our house tired but pleased to be home.

I phoned my mum and she said,

"I've got some sad news for you Harry."

"Oh, what's that then?"

"I'm sorry to tell this but unfortunately your Nan has passed away."

"Oh no. When did that happen?"

"Whilst you were in Holland."

"Really, when is the funeral?"

"It was yesterday."

"Yesterday?"

"Yes."

"You're joking. Why didn't someone tell me?"

"We didn't know where you were staying."

I tried to take in what I'd just been told. I loved my Nan and not being able to say goodbye or be at her funeral was a big thing for me. I was beginning to feel a little upset.

"Okay, mum. Thanks for letting me know. I'll be in touch soon. Take care."

"And you."

I put the phone down and stood there thinking about what I'd just been told. I then went and gave Jayne the bad news."

"Why didn't anyone contact us?"

"Apparently they tried to but they didn't know the number of where we were staying."

"I'm sure that they could have found it out somehow."

"I'm not impressed. I'm going round mum's house now. Do you want to come?"

"No thanks, I'll stay here with the boys."

"Okay, I see you in a bit."

I quickly drove to my parent's house where my mum explained that they tried to get in contact with us but were unable to do so. I appreciated that it was a difficult time but felt that someone in the family would have had the nouse to track me down. Everyone knew the name of the company I worked for so it wouldn't have been too hard to find the number.

My nan was loved by everyone, she was a real character from the North East of England. She lived in Stockton-on-Tees and was a Yorkshire girl having been born in Middlesbrough which was in Yorkshire at the time.

"I'm really disappointed. I'd have come back for her funeral if I'd known about it."

"I know you would Harry but it was just one of those things."

"So, how are you and Dad? Did the funeral go okay?"

"Yes, it all went very well."

"Good, I know it's sad but I bet it was good to see everyone."

"Yes, it was."

"So, are you still up for tonight?"

"I don't think we will be going."

"Why not?"

"We're just feeling a bit tired at the moment."

"That's understandable but we're talking about your brother's Ruby Wedding anniversary. This doesn't happen every day."

"I know but we don't think that we have got the energy to travel up there."

Her brother lived in West London, not that far from Heathrow airport which wasn't the easiest place to get to. They didn't drive so I assumed that they were going to go by train. My Dad still managed to get cheap rail travel.

"I'm really not happy that you are not going. Normally we would give you a lift but as we are taking the boys there isn't enough room in the car."

"I know but maybe next time."

"Next time, when these things come along its important that we support them."

"Okay Harry, I've got to get dinner sorted. I'm glad you had a good time in Holland and love to everyone."

"Thanks mum, take care."

I left them and drove back home. I was still a little in shock myself having just heard the sad news about my lovely Nan but I was really unhappy that they weren't' going to the Ruby wedding celebration tonight.

Jayne was also disappointed but thought that it was their decision and that we should respect that. I wasn't happy and it ate me up all day. I phoned my mum but she was adamant that it they were too tired to go.

I didn't know what to do but, in the end, I came up with a plan.

"Jayne, I've got an idea and would like to run it past you."

"Okay."

"Well, how do you feel if we book a car for mum and dad?"

"What, to take them to London?"

"Yes."

"That will cost a lot."

"I know but I just can't think of another solution."

"Okay, try and find out how much it will cost and we'll discuss it later."

I spent a bit of time on the phone trying to get a good deal. The feedback was that we would need a driver for the evening. He would take mum and dad there and then wait for the party to end and then bring them home. The cost was £90 which was a lot of money but it meant that they would have a comfortable journey.

I told Jayne and she thought that it was a nice thing to do but deep down I think that she felt that it wasn't our problem. I now needed to tell mum and dad, so I drove over and took George with me.

"Just to let you know that a car will be here at 6pm to pick you up and take you to the party."

My mum wasn't happy and my dad remained silent

whilst I let it sink in.

"What about the cost?"

"Don't worry about it, it will be our treat. I've been earning good money in Holland and if you can't treat your parents once in a while then what's the point? Afterall, you've made many sacrifices bringing up three boys over the years."

I was pleased when they relented, and once they agreed to go the mood lightened. Part of me was a little concerned about my dad as he'd been at his Mum's funeral only the day before but I felt that once he met up with everyone and had a beer inside him, he'd be fine.

"Right then, that's sorted. All you need to do now get your 'glad rags' on and we'll see you in London in a short while."

My dad is a very strong character and I don't think I'd ever been that assertive with him over the years but I felt that it was the right thing to do.

*

It was lovely meeting up with all the family, especially as it was for such a nice occasion. My uncle's speech was 'spot on'; it was very entertaining and really did come from the heart. I didn't know that they had met at school all those years ago and had now been married forty years, it was some achievement.

I enjoyed every moment and it was great having George and baby Joseph with us. Sometimes a little adversity in your life makes you appreciate things more than you normally would. I'd been living away from my family for months now and if I was honest with myself, I often felt a little homesick.

Driving back home with the two boys asleep in the back of the car Jayne turned to me and said,

"Did you enjoy your evening dear?"

"Absolutely, it was great seeing everyone."

"Do you think your mum and dad had a good time?"

"Yes, I knew they would once they got chatting and my

dad got a beer or two inside him. It was a little expensive but why not? We don't have enough family get-togethers, especially for such a nice occasion."

"Well, it was only a few weeks ago since Joseph's baptism."

"True. I was a little jealous though."

"Oh, what about?"

"Well, look at it from my parents' point of view. It didn't cost them anything to get there and then they found out that there was an 'open bar' for the whole night. So, they had free booze, free food and then they were driven home by a chauffeur who was paid for by me. I couldn't even have a drink because I'm driving."

"That's the way the cookie crumbles."

"You're not wrong. Anyway, when is the next family get-together?"

"That's going to be my parents ruby wedding anniversary which is in September."

"Crickey, did all of that generation get married in the same year?"

"It appears so."

"So how are your parents going to mark the occasion?"

"They haven't mentioned it at all, but I have a few ideas."

"I'll tell you one thing though; it will be hard to top tonight."

"Yes, it will and I think it was great for your uncle and auntie that your parents were there."

"Absolutely, especially as my dad was their best man…"

***

CHAPTER 16:

EXPENSIVE HOLIDAY.

My first venture into the UK's housing market was nine years earlier when I bought my own place. This was in 1985 and was before I'd met Jayne. I was living with my parents at the time and just thought that it was time to move out.

Being single, and a first-time buyer I was obviously interested in smaller properties. I looked at a lot of different types and being a growing place, Milton Keynes had a really good choice. There was a small cluster of trendy one-bedroomed houses that caught my eye. They were about four years old and had an upstairs 'galleried bedroom' which overlooked the living area which made it feel very spacious.

In the end I had a bit of luck when I spotted a two-bed maisonette that was for sale. Something had gone wrong with its original purchase which was being managed by the local council so they had decided to put it back on the market. I was able to stretch to buying it because of a new 'shared-ownership' scheme that allowed me to buy part of the property and rent the rest from the council.

*

Looking through the local paper each week I'd noticed that there was a one-bedroom houses similar to the ones that I'd looked at years earlier that kept reappearing. Its price had been reduced since I'd first spotted it which was a clue that they really wanted to sell.

The new asking price was £28,000 which was a big drop from the £35,000 that I'd originally seen it advertised for. In the 80's housing boom I knew that these types of houses had peaked at around £60,000, so it really was a bit of a bargain. It reflected the sad state of the housing market and the pain that a lot of people were going through.

We went to view it and it was in excellent condition. The young couple who were selling were about to move into a new-build and my understanding was that they had resorted to selling it to the developer of their new property. It was a sad situation and as we'd had our own housing issues in the past, I knew how they felt.

Jayne wasn't sure that buying a property to rent out was a good idea but I thought that if we could cover our costs the property would surely go up in value and who knows, perhaps over time it could go back up to the dizzy heights of a few years earlier.

I put in a 'cheeky offer' of £25,000 which was immediately rejected. I then increased it by £500 and after a bit of haggling they accepted our offer but this was on the understanding that we would complete the deal as soon as possible. This wasn't a problem because we were cash buyers and didn't have to get a mortgage.

I was pleasantly surprised when they accepted our offer. I was excited about the purchase but also very wary because I didn't know anything about letting out properties. I knew that that there were a few estate agents who had moved into this market so I planned to visit a few on the next weekend that I was back to the UK.

It was perhaps a little naive of me to purchase this house when I didn't even know how much the rental income was going to be but one thing was sure, it was going to be a bit more interesting than putting our money into a boring savings account or buying risky shares.

***

It was decided by the project team that I would support an installation 'on-site' for their 'go-live'. I had only visited one country subsidiary before and that was when we went to Gouda which obviously was our Dutch subsidiary.

This time it was the turn of Belgium and with our offices located in Brussels it was possible to drive there. I got the impression that the usual team had decided to take a break and had therefore just nominated me to do it.

The plan was that I was going to be picked up by one of the team managers at seven o'clock on the Sunday morning. I was pleased that it was the Norwegian chap called Lars whose 30th birthday we'd celebrated earlier in the year.

The company had organised a 'fun day' on the Saturday and I decided to attend. I knew several people and it turned out to be a great day. Unfortunately, we were taken to the location by coach and in the evening, there was going to be a bit of a party. This meant that I was going to get back very late.

We were split into different teams and competed against each other doing lots of interesting and fun activities. Later in the evening I was having a beer when one of the Dutch chaps who was working on the same project as me came over.

"How are you doing Harry?"

"Okay, I'm a bit tired now though. I didn't realise this event was going to go on so long."

"Neither did I."

"I'm being picked up by Lars first thing tomorrow morning and it's going to be very late by the time I get back."

"Do you want a lift? I'm driving so I can take you if you want me to."

"That's very kind of you. When are you planning on leaving?"

"Probably at about ten."

"Okay, I'll go with you. It will mean that I will still get home late but at least I won't have to wait around for the coach."

It was probably around 11pm when I got home and I fell asleep straightaway.

***

Lars picked me up spot on 7am. He had also been at the event the day before and to this day one of my everlasting memories of him is wrestling with another chap whilst wearing a fake 'sumo' outfit.

I was pleased that he was driving. He was obviously more experienced at driving in Europe than I was. We got there in no time and were met by a member of the finance team who was going to have the final say on whether we were going to go live or not.

We set to work with the installation and once it was finished, we expected to be able to start the long drive back to Holland. However, rather than accept that what we had done was correct he wanted to produce some invoices on the production system.

We agreed and he was happy with the results. I thought that this test would be the end of the matter but he said that he wanted his test invoices removed from the system.

I looked at Lars and he looked at me, we weren't expecting to have to do this. Lars turned to the chap and said,

"Can't you just void the invoices?"

"No, because they have been allocated a number and we will need to allocate this number to an actual invoice."

He was adamant that the test invoices needed to be erased from the system so that there was no trace of them ever existing. I was annoyed that the implementation plan hadn't been better thought through. We shouldn't have been asked to do this without being informed first so that we could have prepared for it.

Lars phoned one of our managers but he didn't know what to do either. Lars then said,

"It is possible to get some lunch somewhere, I think we need to work out how we are going to deal with this situation."

"Everything around here is closed on Sundays."

"Is there nowhere where we can get a burger or even a sandwich?"

"The only place that I can think of that is open is the airport."

"Okay, you two go and get what you can. I need to make a few phone calls."

I turned to Lars and said,

"If we can't fix this then we are going to have to do a restore and do the whole implementation again."

"I know Harry but I'm not sure if anyone is available to help."

Driving through Brussels I tried to think about how we could get out of our current predicament. Our Belgian host was adamant that his test invoices needed to be removed so we needed to come up with a plan and quickly.

We managed to get some ham and cheese rolls from a shop at the airport and then made our way back to the office. I'd used the system for many years and had a couple of tricks up my sleeve but was wary of doing this in a production environment.

"Hi Lars, have you had any ideas?"

"They seem to think that you should be able to remove the entries directly in the database."

"I've been thinking about that. It's not as straightforward as you think and is extremely risky. You need to remember that this is a production system. It would be very easy for me to delete the wrong entries and then we would have no choice but to do a restore."

"Well, that's the only option on the table at the moment."

"Okay then, I'll give it a go. Can you give me the invoice numbers please?"

I knew my way around the database tables and it was easy enough for me to delete the entries. There were only two tables, one for the invoice header records and one for the line items associated with each of the headers.

"Right, I've done that but I don't know how we are going to test it."

The Belgium then said that he had some live invoices that we could put through the system. I was dumfounded, why didn't he do that in the first place instead of creating test ones and then telling us that we had to remove them?

He created a brand-new invoice and all the values appeared correct but he wasn't happy with the invoice number.

"This number is the next number in the sequence after the two dummy invoices were raised. It should be the same number as the first dummy invoice that we created this morning."

I was getting a little irate now but I remembered when I worked in the Munich office between Christmas and New Year that I'd spent some time looking into this area when I was testing one of my programs.

"Can you give me a moment; I want to try something?"

"Sure."

I logged on to my account on the Munich test system and after some digging around, I found a test program that I'd developed. This never made it into production and I'd created it just to help me test another program.

Looking at the code it all came straight back to me. I quickly reset the invoice numbers and then deleted the database table entries for the invoice that he had just created. He then recreated the production invoice and to everyone's relief it looked correct.

There was nothing more to be done so Lars and I bade farewell to our Belgium host and started our drive back to Holland. Driving up the motorway I shut my eyes. I was exhausted, I'd enjoyed the 'fun day' but getting back so late had taken its toll on me.

I thought that I was just going to be making up the numbers on Belgium's go-live but in the end, I found myself 'hacking' the system. I was pleased that I'd learnt how to do it earlier in the year but was annoyed that it was down to me to fix a production system in this way.

***

Jayne phoned me up,

"Harry, I want to go on holiday and you definitely need a holiday."

"Okay, but I'm not sure that they will allow me any time off at the moment."

"When was the last time we had a two-week holiday?"

"Umm, I can't remember. Probably when we took the tent to Cornwall."

"Yes, and that was before we moved to Scotland and well before the two boys arrived, so it must be over four years ago."

"Okay, but I'm not sure that they are going to like it."

"I cannot believe that you can't take any holiday. It's ridiculous, expecting people to work like this. They wouldn't expect you to work all these hours if you were a permanent employee, would they?"

Jayne had a point; her life was difficult too as she was living on her own with two very young boys to look after. I was now getting pressure from two sides, my workplace and my wife. I just didn't know what to do.

In the end, I decided to email my boss requesting a holiday. I wasn't sure how this was going to be accepted but I had to try.

I remembered how difficult they made things for me when Joseph was due to be born was troubling me. I needed a firm commitment so I decided to 'go in a little harder' this time.

In the email I stated that I wanted a two-week holiday and if this wasn't granted then I wouldn't renew my contract which was up for renewal in the next couple of weeks (not that I had a written contract).

I knew that this was a bit strong but I felt that it was time to make a bit of a stand. There was no point in Jayne booking something only to be told that we couldn't go.

The next day I arrived at work and made my way to my desk. Once I booted my PC up, I could see that I had an email from my boss who was working at a subsidiary location at the time.

It was a long email and I read it as quickly as I could, trying to see if he'd granted me my holiday.

One of my Dutch colleagues came over and asked me to look into something for him. He was very persistent but I wasn't in the mood to help him out.

"Do you mind if you wait a moment? I need to read this email. It's important to me."

I could see that he wasn't impressed but fortunately, he gave in,

"I'll give you a few minutes Harry."

"Thanks, it won't take long."

I read the email and then I read it again. My boss had granted me the holiday but he'd made sure that he had is say.

Working there for the past eight months, I should have known that they weren't going to be dictated to by me. He obviously didn't like what I'd said and he pointed out that I needed to understand that the work had to be done.

I stared at my PC in disbelief at what I'd just read. I'd given my all on this project and now I was reading the biggest pile of crap I'd ever read in my life. The Dutch chap came over again but there was no way I was the right state of mind to talk to him, let alone help him out.

"Look, you're a good bloke but right now I'd really appreciate it if you could give me a little space. We're friends and normally I would help you out but please leave me alone right now."

I think he sensed that I was a little upset,

"Okay Harry, whenever you're ready."

I could feel my blood beginning to boil. The anger was welling up in me like a gushing Icelandic geyser. It was all consuming and I knew I was going to blow.

Somehow, I managed to control myself. I went over and picked up my bag and started to walk towards the stairs. I could feel everyone looking at me but I didn't care. I didn't care about anything anymore I just knew that I needed to get out of the building.

No-one said a word and I quickly went down the stairs. Walking along the main corridor on the ground floor there was one word that I'd read that I just couldn't get out of my head.

"How dare he? How bloody dare he?"

Someone I knew came the other way but I just looked down at the carpet so that I didn't make eye contact. I didn't want to talk to anyone. That one word just kept repeating in my head.

"How dare he? How bloody dare he?"

He had given in to my request for a holiday but he'd obviously felt that he had done so under duress. I assumed that this was because of my threat of not renewing my contract. Perhaps I shouldn't have said that but I felt that it was the only bargaining position that I had. In his email he stated,

"I feel that I have to give into your blackmail."

"BLACKMAIL..."

How dare he call me a blackmailer because I wanted to go on holiday with my wife and children; the bastard.

I reached the main entrance and looked over to my left at the pretty Dutch girl on reception. She looked up and smiled. This disarmed me a little but I was still struggling to control of my emotions. I casually walked over to her and said,

"I'm not sure if you are aware but this is my last day here today."

She looked at me with a little confused expression on her face. Normally there is a set protocol when people left companies and I knew that they were often escorted off the premises by management or HR.

I put my hand in my pocket and pulled out my security badge and placed it on the desk right in front of her. I could see that she was still a little confused and didn't know what to do.

"I'd be grateful if you could see that this gets sent to the correct place."

"Sure, I'll see to it."

"That's very kind of you."

I then turned and walked towards the revolving doors but before I got there, I did a pirouette and blew a kiss which I aimed at all the good peopled I'd worked with. I then went through the doors and out into the fresh air.

*

It was still early in the morning as I made my way back towards my apartment. When I got there, I packed as quickly as I could. I wrote a quick message to Duncan thanking him for everything but due to unforeseen circumstances I was leaving Holland today.

There was no way that I could take all of my belongings home in one go, so I said that I would be back to collect the rest very soon. This was annoying because there was no way that I wanted to come back but I had no choice.

My head was spinning so I decided to make myself a cup of tea. I was still so angry but I didn't regret what I'd done. I just wanted to get home as quickly as I could. I didn't want to see or speak to anyone and I knew that I wouldn't be able to relax until I was back on home soil.

Looking out of the window I spotted Lars, he was looking around and I assumed that he was looking for me. I was trapped, Lars was a really good chap and I liked him a lot but I didn't want to speak to him. I decided to keep away from the windows and being on the fourth floor I was sure that he wouldn't be able to see me.

I sat there waiting for the doorbell to chime or worse

still the apartment door to open. I don't know if they'd contacted Duncan or not. I wanted to make a break for it but there was only one way in and one way out. It gave me time to think a little and I knew in my heart that there was no going back.

If I'd kept my badge, I could have easily come up with some story about not feeling very well and no-one would be any the wiser but to go back and say that I'd made a mistake was now impossible.

I remembered an old Army Sergeant saying to me once, "If you're going to go AWOL make sure you have your ID card with you. If you don't have your ID card with you then you can be done for desertion and under military law that can still warrants the death sentence."

So, there was no going back. Well, not without losing face and I wasn't prepared to do that.

Fifteen minutes or so must have passed before I thought that it would now be safe for me to make my move. I slowly opened the door and listened out for any sound. I then carried my two suitcases to the lift and went back and shut the apartment door.

The lift doors opened on the ground floor and again I waited but couldn't hear anyone so I made my way to the front door and listened. Again, I couldn't hear anything so I gingerly opened the door and looked around. It was spookily quiet; there just didn't seem to be anyone about so I locked the door and walked up the path dragging my two wheeled suitcases behind me.

Walking to the station I felt like a prisoner 'on the run' which in some ways I was. My paranoia tendencies were on overdrive and I thought that at any moment my boss would leap out of the bushes and drag me back to solitary confinement which was my desk.

My lifestyle had a lot of similarities to that of a prisoner but my jailer had been money and not a prison guard. If I did bump into anyone, I was pretty sure that I could out run them but I'd have to leave my two suitcases behind.

*

The train stopped at Delft and it bought back memories of a lovely morning we'd spent there. That seemed like a lifetime ago now and I knew that my life was never going to be the same again.

I booked a flight to Heathrow and felt safe once I was on the plane. I didn't really know what I was afraid of because there was nothing to be afraid of; I guess that it was just the state of my mind at the time. I suppose having been 'controlled' as tightly as I had been, I was subconsciously 'conditioned' to think that this was normal and that I wasn't allowed to do anything for myself.

Flying over London bought back fond memories of the marathon. I'd done it twice now which gave me a connection with the city that I hadn't had before. It was like we had a subconscious bond that I still feel today.

It wasn't long before I was waiting for the tube to go to Euston and when I got there, I felt that I had to make the phone call.

"Hi Jayne, its me."

"Oh, this is a surprise. How are you?"

"Umm, I've been better."

"What do you mean?"

"Well, I received a response for my holiday request."

"And, is he going to allow it?"

"Yes, but unfortunately he didn't word it very diplomatically and I got so angry that I just got up and walked out."

"You walked out!"

"Yes. I'm at Euston station now and will be home in an hour and a half I guess."

"Why did you walk out if he granted you your holiday? That doesn't make sense to me."

"Well, he sent a very long email in which he made a lot of points but there was one thing that I just couldn't handle."

"And what was that?"

"He said that he would 'give in to my blackmail' and I really don't think I deserved to be spoken to like that."

"Blackmail! How did you blackmail him?"

"All I said was that if he didn't grant me a holiday then I wouldn't renew my contract."

"I must admit that that does sound a bit 'heavy handed' Harry."

"Well, do you remember how badly they treated me when Joseph was born? I didn't want them to mess me around like that again. We didn't know whether or not I was going to make to the birth; it was outrageous."

"Well, it looks to me like there's no going back now."

"I know."

"Okay, I understand why you've done this and you know very well that I will support you, especially after all we've been through but I will tell you one thing Harry."

"What's that Jayne?"

"You know that I love you and you are welcome to come home."

"Yes."

"Well, when you get here, you better not be a miserable bastard!"

She then hung up!

*** THE END ***